J.G. Ballard

Landscapes of Tomorrow

Edited by

Richard Brown
Christopher Duffy
Elizabeth Stainforth

BRILL
RODOPI

LEIDEN | BOSTON

Cover illustration: Fay Ballard, "Car in Desert Photograph", detail from Memory Box: About my Father, pencil on Bockingford paper (2012).

The Library of Congress Cataloging-in-Publication Data is available online at http://catalog.loc.gov
LC record available at http://lccn.loc.gov/2016022436

Want or need Open Access? Brill Open offers you the choice to make your research freely accessible online in exchange for a publication charge. Review your various options on brill.com/brill-open.

Typeface for the Latin, Greek, and Cyrillic scripts: "Brill". See and download: brill.com/brill-typeface.

ISSN 1574-9630
ISBN 978-90-04-31385-9 (hardback)
ISBN 978-90-04-31386-6 (e-book)

Printed by Printforce, United Kingdom

Contents

Standard Abbreviations for Editions of Primary Texts by Ballard used in This Volume

Dates of first publication are given in square brackets where these differ from the editions used.

Ballard, J.G. *The Drowned World*. [New York: Berkley, 1962]. London: Fourth Estate, 2014. *DW*

Ballard, J.G. *The Atrocity Exhibition*. [London: Jonathan Cape, 1970]. London: Fourth Estate, 2014. *AE*

Ballard, J.G. *Crash*. [London: Jonathan Cape, 1973]. London: Fourth Estate, 2014. *C*

Ballard, J.G. *Vermilion Sands*. [London: Jonathan Cape, 1973]. London: Vintage, 2001. *VS*

Ballard, J.G. *High-Rise*. [London: Jonathan Cape, 1975]. London: Fourth Estate, 2014. *HR*

Ballard, J.G. *Hello America*. [London: Jonathan Cape, 1981]. London: Fourth Estate, 2104. *HA*

Ballard, J.G. *J.G. Ballard*. Edited by V. Vale and Andrea Juno. San Francisco: Re/Search Publications, 1984. *R/S JGB*

Ballard, J.G. *Empire of the Sun*. [London: Victor Gollancz, 1984]. London: Fourth Estate, 2014. *ES*

Ballard, J.G. *The Day of Creation*. [London: Victor Gollancz, 1987]. London: Fourth Estate, 2014. *DC*

Ballard, J.G. *The Kindness of Women*. [London: HarperCollins, 1991]. London: Fourth Estate, 2014. *KW*

Ballard, J.G. *Rushing to Paradise*. [London: Flamingo, 1994]. London: Fourth Estate, 2014. *RP*

Ballard, J.G. *A User's Guide to the Millennium: Essays and Reviews*. London: Flamingo, 1996. *UGM*

Ballard, J.G. *Super-Cannes*. [London: Flamingo, 2000]. London: Fourth Estate, 2014. *SC*

Ballard, J.G. *The Complete Short Stories: Volume 1*. [London: Flamingo, 2001]. London: Fourth Estate, 2014. *CSS1*

Ballard, J.G. *The Complete Short Stories: Volume 2*. [London: Flamingo, 2001]. London: Fourth Estate, 2014. *CSS2*

Ballard, J.G. "The Day of Reckoning". *The New Statesman*, 4 July 2005. http://www.new-statesman.com/200507040040, accessed 20 April 2015. *DR*

Ballard, J.G. *Kingdom Come*. [London: Fourth Estate, 2006]. London: Fourth Estate, 2014. *KC*

Ballard, J.G. *Miracles of Life: An Autobiography*. London: Harper Perennial, 2008. *ML*

Ballard, J.G. *Extreme Metaphors: Interviews With J.G. Ballard, 1967–2008*. Edited by Simon Sellars and Dan O'Hara. London: Fourth Estate, 2012. *EM*

Notes on Contributors

Jeannette Baxter
teaches modern and contemporary literature at Anglia Ruskin University, Cambridge. She is the author of *J.G. Ballard's Surrealist Imagination: Spectacular Authorship* (Ashgate 2009); editor of *J.G. Ballard: Contemporary Critical Perspectives* (Bloomsbury 2008); and co-editor of *Visions and Revisions: Essays on J.G. Ballard* (Palgrave 2012); *Women A Cultural Review: Reading Jean Rhys* (Routledge 2012); and *A Literature of Restitution: Critical Essays on W.G. Sebald* (Manchester 2013). She is Series Co-Editor of *Contemporary Critical Perspectives* (Bloomsbury), and is writing a monograph entitled *Exquisite Corpse: Literature/Surrealisms/Fascisms*.

Richard Brown
is Reader in Modern Literature in the School of English at the University of Leeds and the author of academic work on James Joyce including *James Joyce: A Postculturalist Perspective* (Palgrave Macmillan, 1992), *Joyce, "Penelope" and the Body* (Rodopi, 2006) and *A Companion to James Joyce* (Blackwell, 2008) as well as on contemporary writers including Ian McEwan and Bob Dylan. His essay "Reading J.G. Ballard After the Millennium: the Scars of *Crash, Cocaine Nights* and *Millennium People*" appeared in the *Millennial Fictions* special issue of *Critical Engagements* Volume 2, No. 2 (Autumn/Winter 2008), 125–149.

Christopher Duffy
has a PhD from the School of English at the University of Leeds. His thesis is titled "Heterotopic Space in Selected Works of J.G. Ballard." He received his BA in History from the University of Manchester and MA in Modern to Contemporary Literature from the University of Leeds.

William Fingleton
is a doctoral candidate at University College Dublin, where he also took his undergraduate and MA programs. His thesis is a psychological approach the literature of Ballard, under the working title of "J.G. Ballard: Psyence Fiction."

Thomas Knowles
has a PhD from Nottingham Trent University. His thesis is entitled "Lyrical Ballards: The Wounded Romanticism of J.G. Ballard." He co-edited and contributed a chapter to a book called *Insanity and the Lunatic Asylum in the Nineteenth Century* (Routledge, 2014), and a chapter for *Supernatural and*

the Gothic Tradition (McFarland, 2016). He teaches Gothic, Victorian and Twentieth-Century literature at Birmingham City University.

Graham Matthews

is Associate Professor in Literature at Nanyang Technological University, Singapore. He is the author of *Ethics and Desire in the Wake of Postmodernism* (Bloomsbury 2012), *Will Self and Contemporary British Society* (Palgrave Macmillan 2015), and (with Sam Goodman) the editor of *Violence and the Limits of Representation* (Palgrave Macmillan 2013) as well as contributions to various journals and edited collections on contemporary literature.

Catherine McKenna

is a doctoral candidate at King's College, London, researching the work of J.G. Ballard. She has worked with the J.G. Ballard Estate to catalogue Ballard's private library collection, and this collection now forms a central part of her research. Her research examines the role of Ballard's library in his work, with a particular emphasis on the theme of mediation.

Guglielmo Poli

is currently a doctoral candidate at the University of Genova, working on a thesis about the poetics of ambiguity in J.G. Ballard's work. He is especially interested in an interdisciplinary approach to this topic involving the interplay with neurosciences and cognitive studies.

Elizabeth Stainforth

is a doctoral candidate in the School of Fine Art History of Art and Cultural Studies at the University of Leeds. Her research explores memory's significance for cultural heritage, in the wake of digital technologies. Her undergraduate dissertation on *The Atrocity Exhibition* led to an interest in Ballard's collaborations with Eduardo Paolozzi in *Ambit*, culminating in an exhibition at the Henry Moore Institute in 2011. She received the Institute's MA prize for her essay, "'A Revelation of Unexpected Associations': J.G. Ballard, Eduardo Paolozzi and Helen Chadwick in *Ambit*." Recently, she has worked with Mike Bonsall on "The Invisible Library" project, which is hosted on the *Digital Ballard* website.

Andrew Warstat

is a lecturer in media theory at Manchester Metropolitan University. He is a writer, photographer and artist. Exhibitions include *After the Disaster* (Outpost, 2008) and *The Object of Photography* (The Stanley & Audrey Burton Gallery, 2009). He is co-editor of the journal *Fieldworks*. Recent publications include essays on John Stezaker (*parallax,* 2010), the role of ignorance and "self reading" in contemporary art (*On Not Knowing: How Artists Think,* Blackdog Publishing, 2013) and on the filmmaker Lewis Klahr (Edinburgh University Press, forthcoming).

Introduction

The ten essays that make up *J.G. Ballard: Landscapes of Tomorrow* address various kinds of landscapes in Ballard's writing and respond to the "spatial turn" in the arts and humanities, which opens a rich new vista for the reading of narrative fiction. Often informed by interdisciplinary and theoretical approaches, the themes explored here re-cast the concept of the spatial at the same time as grounding their analysis in it. For such analysis the fiction of J.G. Ballard immediately recommends itself. Landscapes and spatiality are crucial to Ballard's imagination though not in an unmediated or straightforwardly naturalistic sense. Whether environmental, cultural, psychological, digital or political, landscapes inform the approaches to his work which follow.

In 1968, fascinated by the new kind of science fiction Ballard was producing, the Danish poet Jannick Storm commented: "Well, this is why your landscapes are not real, I suppose. They are sort of symbolic." Ballard replied:

> Well, they are not real in the sense that I don't write naturalistically about the present day. Though, in the latest group of stories I've started to write, these stories written in paragraph form, which I call 'condensed novels,' there I'm using the landscape of the present day. The chief characters in these stories are people like Elizabeth Taylor, Marilyn Monroe, Jacqueline Kennedy and so on. There I'm using present-day landscapes. Obviously if you're going to set most of your fiction several years ahead of the present, you're going to have to use an invented landscape to some extent, because you can't write naturalistically about London or New York twenty years from now. It must be an invented landscape to a certain extent.
>
> *EM* 16

Ballard here contrasts the "invented landscape" of future-oriented fictions with the "landscape of the present day" that is the subject of the condensed novels in *The Atrocity Exhibition* (1970), thereby acknowledging that those landscapes too form part of the imaginative project of his work. That text provides the centre point of this volume, being the main focus of three of the essays and a point of reference for all the others. Among Ballard's works its various landscapes are some of the most challenging and extensive and consequently inform the range of approaches to all the texts taken here. Ballard's landscapes may be "invented" yet his readers and critics are well aware that his landscapes of the present are no more "naturalistic" than the invented landscapes of the future. His fiction famously re-orientates the conventional science-fiction landscapes of outer space to those of "inner space." In his own words, "landscape is a

© KONINKLIJKE BRILL NV, LEIDEN, 2016 | DOI 10.1163/9789004313866_002 formalization of space and time. And the external landscapes directly reflect interior states of mind" (*EM* 5). "In literature," as Margaret Atwood puts it, "every landscape is a state of mind, but every state of mind can also be portrayed by a landscape" (*In Other Worlds* 75).

In the notes that Ballard wrote to accompany *The Atrocity Exhibition*, he introduces the phrase "media landscape" (*AE* 37, 145, 163), thereby adding a third and no less significant dimension to the configurations of the landscapes of tomorrow that are imagined in the fiction and discussed in the essays in this collection. Ballard's prescient analyses of our landscapes of culture and information have done much to drive the increased awareness of the contemporary relevance and urgency of his work. Alongside classic theorists of the spatial turn since Joseph Frank, such as Fredric Jameson, Edward Soja, Henri Lefebvre and Michel Foucault, critics here assembled draw on a range of other writers and theorists to help map these landscapes, including thinkers as diverse as Marx, Freud, R.D. Laing, Alfred Korzybski, Gregory Bateson and Marc Augé.

Fredric Jameson's recognition, developed in *Archaeologies of the Future*, that significant challenges are still posed to critical recuperation by science-fiction and speculative literatures, is gradually being more widely accepted in academic circles, as the traumatic birth of one new century gives way to our need to imagine the futures of the next. Works such as David James's *Contemporary British Fiction and the Artistry of Space* demonstrate the validity of spatial approaches across the contemporary fictional sphere. Ballard's work is an especially rich and fertile field in these respects.

The fragmentary structure of *The Atrocity Exhibition* produces multiple potential narratives and a series of cultural landscapes embedded with different levels of literary and spatial reference. It is Ballard's most challenging and experimental book, developing themes from his earlier disaster novels and prefiguring some of his later, most celebrated and discussed works in which many of the psychological, social and political insights it traces are embodied more fully. In this collection, earlier texts such as *The Drowned World* (1962), "The Terminal Beach" (1964), "The Dead Astronaut" (1968) and *Vermilion Sands* (first published as a collection in 1971) that establish many of the recurrent ideas in *The Atrocity Exhibition* are discussed. Their transformed post-apocalyptic environments appear also as emerging landscapes of memory. Essays in the middle section consider *The Atrocity Exhibition* itself in the context of various cultural landscapes, including the influence of literary modernism and collections of ephemera termed invisible literature. The final section traces Ballard's continuing fascination with the themes of *The Atrocity Exhibition*, concentrating on the distinctive physical and psychological landscapes described in three of his more recent dystopian texts: *Crash* (1973) whose material most directly emerges from *The Atrocity Exhibition*; *High-Rise* (1975) and *Kingdom Come* (2006).

Different kinds of space and different spatial concepts underpin the essays collected here, from the landscapes of Ballard's youth in Shanghai and his writing life in suburban London, to nuclear testing spaces (notably, the Pacific Islands) and the exploration of outer space. Also discussed are the figurative locations typical of Ballard's work: the beach, the motorway, the high-rise and the shopping mall. Textual spaces are explored through Ballard's affiliation with modernist and other literary forms, including surrealist prose writing, collage, and poetic romanticism. Likewise, examination of Ballard's use of what he calls invisible literature, such as the photographic records of nuclear testing and medical accounts of crash injuries, voice an emerging area of scholarship for Ballard studies.

The interdisciplinary range of the volume includes literature, visual cultures, fine art, archival studies, digital humanities, politics and sociology. The geographical reach is also broad, with contributions from British, Continental European and China-based scholars, writers and academics, including an imaginative contribution from one of Ballard's two daughters, the artist Fay Ballard, whose recent exhibition *House Clearance* (Eleven Spitalfields Gallery, 2014) drew richly on her father's legacy.

Fay Ballard's "Shanghai/Shepperton" is a piece of imaginative writing which fittingly opens the volume by expressing the complex layering of familiar and distant places that was such a remarkable feature of Ballard's childhood. Her work might be thought to inform the fascinations with landscape in Ballard's work, familiarizing the distant and exotic, and distancing the familiarity of suburbia at the same time.

In the chapter which follows, Graham Matthews richly develops this position, arguing that, though set in London, *The Drowned World* recalls the landscape of Shanghai where Ballard lived until he was sixteen. Matthews shows that Ballard recalls post-war Shanghai as a place filled with abandoned buildings, empty swimming pools and collapsed irrigation systems. This is reflected in the novel, where descriptions of the Ritz are more reminiscent of Shanghai's Peace Hotel and repeated references to bamboo groves, lush vegetation, huge rivers, canals, and flooded paddy fields also recall Shanghai. Just as characters in the novel steadily regress into primordial forms, *The Drowned World* reaches back to Ballard's own archaeopsychic past: "[P]erhaps these sunken lagoons simply remind me of the drowned world of my uterine childhood" (*DW* 28) the scientist-protagonist Kerans speculates. Matthews's chapter draws extensively on historical representations of China in the 1930s and 1940s, allowing for a discussion of the relationship between real and fictional English and

Chinese landscapes and how these are re-visioned through memory and imagination. For Ballard, historical events cannot be remembered with certainty and instead "truth" is found in the elaborate fictions that awaken affective responses to the landscape. Shanghai and London are locations that embody these distinct positions since, in Ballard's fiction, Shanghai's dramatic scenes of war and natural disaster differ sharply from the banality and parochialism of the English landscape.

By contrast, Thomas Knowles finds traces of a familiar cultural landscape in the apparently fantastical and otherworldly settings that are laid out in the stories that make up *Vermilion Sands*. His chapter addresses the beach, another of the symbolic spaces which recur in Ballard's work, and the strange Ballardian condition of "beach fatigue." His argument further extends the textual dimensions of the spatial realm, exploring the little-noted legacy of English literary Romanticism in the stories. Drawing on such canonical sources as Wordsworth's "Preface" to *Lyrical Ballads* and the academic literary criticism of M.H. Abrams, it reads the sonic sculptures and singing statues of *Vermilion Sands* as postmodern transformations of the Romantic Aeolian lyre, played by the wind and by the lamia-like muses that figure in each story. The legacy of the glimpse of Romanticism in these stories, he suggests, is reworked into the beach-like location of "The Summer Cannibals" section of *The Atrocity Exhibition*.

Catherine McKenna's "Zones of Non-Time" brings the textual landscape out of the traditionally literary and into the world of contemporary news and information media, tracing the residues of some of the iconic media events that recur in Ballard's writing to the extensive or even bizarre range of information sources that inspired his work. Ballard left a private library collection whose materials form a landscape of influence and inspiration. McKenna's essay selects two items from this collection which mark the cultural experience of the twentieth century as presented in Ballard: the advent of the atomic bomb in the unnerving landscape of the nuclear testing site and the hauntingly replayed location of the assassination of John F. Kennedy.

Andrew Warstat's reading of "The Dead Astronaut," Ballard's short story that is a rare foray into the futuristic territory of space travel, captures the relocation from outer to inner space, since he argues that in it we find a "stalled future" in which a failed process of mourning suggests the "disappearance of tomorrow." For Warstat, the protagonist's return to this stalled future is approachable through the account of the mourning process in Freudian and post-Freudian psychology. It is characterized by the impossibility or absence of a primal scene. Instead of productively mourning one particular version of the future, the story reiterates a traumatic process of *nachträglichkeit* or "coming after." In this respect it allows Warstat to ask whether the text embodies the interminable stasis of post-modernity or else becomes an allegory of the intensifying processes of commodification in modernity.

In the first of the essays on *The Atrocity Exhibition* itself, Richard Brown selects two examples of the intertextual to inform a discussion of the landscape of apocalyptic intertextuality which we find in Ballard's work. The first is the story by Alfred Jarry "The Crucifixion Considered as an Uphill Bicycle Race," which is recast with close similarity to the original in the fifteenth chapter of the book. This is typical of Ballard's turn for inspiration to the historical *avant-garde* of the early twentieth century and especially here to a notable precursor of Surrealism for whom the irrational holds out the best hope of an explanation of an irrational world. The second example is found in the fascinating, profound, complex and sometimes contradictory admiration expressed by Ballard for the work of James Joyce, who, like Ballard, found himself a hero of many *avant-garde* movements whilst retaining his independence from all of them. Brown unearths intriguing aspects of Joyce's deep presence in *The Atrocity Exhibition* and elsewhere in Ballard.

The second essay on *The Atrocity Exhbition* itself is by Guglielmo Poli whose chapter focuses on the landscape of meaning and perception in the text, offering an extended discussion of the relation of the map to its territory that is formulated in the phrase "the map is not the territory," quoted by Ballard in *Empire of the Sun* (1984). Poli explains that this phrase was coined by the Polish mathematician Alfred Korzybski and later developed by the British anthropologist Gregory Bateson, who theorized about a system able to demonstrate the natural world's unity as a result of the formal relations that constitute it. In *The Atrocity Exhibition* the reader is introduced to the strange world of protagonists who attempt to make up a picture of the world constituted by a geometry of relations between objects divested of their normal functions and emotional resonances. The characters' search for meaning is an attempt to understand the configuration of this imaginary geometry, which owes something to Korzybski and Bateson, and is illuminated by an examination of the inseparability of the mind and its materials and the Jungian distinction between *creatura* and *pleroma*.

In the third essay on the text, "'The Logic of the Visible at the Service of the Invisible': Reading Invisible Literature in *The Atrocity Exhibition*," Elizabeth Stainforth adventurously explores the textual landscapes of the book, highlighting and developing the concept of invisible literature, which was Ballard's own term for different kinds of marginal reading material which populate and inform his work. This invisible literature, examples of which include scientific reports, company brochures and advertising leaflets, form the materials of a collage technique, which he adopts from the practices of Surrealism. For Ballard the art movement was the first to place "the logic of the visible at the service of the invisible" and these invisible literatures are used by Ballard to further his exploration of the alternative psychic realities of inner space. Ballard's invisible literature also presents a substantial challenge to the established conventions of cultural memory and to the preservation of the archive, to which the innovative digital archiving project accompanying the essay responds.

In his essay "Hidden Heterotopias in *Crash*," Christopher Duffy visits those motorway landscapes which originate in the scientific and cultural experiments of *The Atrocity Exhibition* and become embodied in the lived world of Ballard's most controversial dystopia, *Crash*. These landscapes are distinctively decoded through the spatial theories of Michel Foucault and Marc Augé as rebellious enclaves established within the motorway space. They may resemble Michel Foucault's heterotopias of illusion which work to show up the enclosure and partitioning of the more actively governed spaces that surround them. One such enclave is the personalized car cabin itself which in this novel becomes a rebellious site effectively hidden from the controlling gaze of authority. Duffy argues that *Crash* does more than critique the motorized landscapes of modernity. It defiantly re-appropriates the motorway as a radically experimental space open to different kinds of access that challenge proscriptive and officially sanctioned use.

The recognition that Ballardian landscapes represent a necessary conjuncture of psychological and political dimensions runs throughout these essays. Such conjunctures are fundamental to William Fingleton's chapter "Pillars of the Community: The Tripartite Characterization of *High-Rise*," which re-reads the architectural spaces of that novel of 1975, which is currently enjoying a new audience thanks to the 2015 Ben Wheatley film version. For Fingleton, it is characterization, as much as physical space, which provides the key to the landscape of this novel in that Wilder, Laing and Royal, the three residents of his increasingly psychopathic tower block, can be understood as representatives of different forms of class consciousness, as different parts of Freud's cognitive model, or as archetypal exemplars of the three psychological conditions of pronoia, paranoia and metanoia.

In conclusion, Jeannette Baxter's essay on Ballard's last novel, *Kingdom Come* (2006), finds in its symbolic landscape a direct recall of De Chirico's "nowhere" landscape as imagined in his painting *The Disquieting Muses* first painted in 1916 and his little-read 1926 novel *Hebdomeros*. She argues that Ballard takes up this Surrealist "nowhere" motif in order to intimate the survival of disparate forms of fascism in contemporary history, politics and culture, from the soft-totalitarianism forged by the illusion of consumerist choice, to the neo-fascist communities that commit racially-motivated acts of violence against displaced, immigrant workers. Baxter's challenging and provocative essay selects an example of Ballard's landscapes from the remarkable late flourishing of his fictional career in the first years of this century. It grounds his political critique of the contemporary in his deep engagement with the historical *avant-garde* and makes its political implications for our immediate future world unnervingly explicit.

Baxter's chapter originally formed the keynote paper at the conference *J.G. Ballard: Landscapes of Tomorrow*, which took place in the Stanley & Audrey Burton Gallery and the School of English at the University of Leeds in May 2014, with the additional support of the Business Confucius Institute at the University. Not all of the papers presented at the conference found a home in the collection and in some cases those that did have developed their intellectual journeys through the Ballardian landscape since that time. Among those not able to be present on that occasion, we would especially like to acknowledge the invaluable interest and support of Bea Ballard. The collaborative and interdisciplinary spirit of the conference remains everywhere apparent in this volume which is offered as a tribute to the enduring and developing dynamism and relevance of Ballard's work in the rapidly shifting and advancing critical, intellectual and research landscapes of tomorrow's worlds.

Works Cited

Atwood, Margaret. "Dire Cartographies: the Roads to Ustopia" in *In Other Worlds: Science Fiction and the Human Imagination*. London: Virago, 2011. 66–96.

Ballard, Fay. *House Clearance*. Published by the artist in connection with the exhibition "House Clearance" Eleven Spitalfields Gallery, London, 2014.

James, David. *Contemporary British Fiction and the Artistry of Space*. London: Continuum, 2008.

Jameson, Fredric. *Archaeologies of the Future*. London: Verso, 2005.

Shanghai/*Shepperton*

Shanghai, intense light. Cicadas scream. *Shepperton, electric lights always on in high summer.* Forty degrees and humid. *Fan heaters on full at home.* Neoclassical, creamy white Shanghai Hospital. Born. *Chiswick House, neo-Palladian, white. Shepperton Memorial.* Shanghai Hospital: green lawns, firs and magnolia trees. *Green lawns of Shepperton.*

Ballard, H G Wells. Johnstone, bridge and tennis. Paris of the East: international sophistication, violence, unfetted capitalism, death and acute poverty. Anything is possible, no limits to human imagination. Freud. 31 Amherst Ave, substantial English mock-tudor. *Suburban Surrey, polished parquet floors. Grandmother's home, neighbours' homes.* Roast beef, Coca Cola.

Amherst Ave surrounding fields and canals. *Shepperton surrounding fields* and *rivers, the splash.* Whangpoo river annual flood. *River Thames at Twickenham, Richmond and Shepperton. Reservoirs, gravel pits.* Swimming pools.

Amherst garden, lawn, shrubs, deciduous trees. Rhododendrons. *Shepperton, lawns and gardens.* Tropical palms and bamboos. *Overgrown Shepperton garden. The yucca.*

Amherst neighbour's kitchen: black and white checkerboard tiles, painted wooden cupboards, double doors of opaque bubble glass, wooden dresser, ceramic sink. *Almost identical to Shepperton kitchen. Time stops still. No DIY.*

Cathedral School for Boys, black steeple. Latin grammar and scriptures. Ely School and Kings. Dissection. Intimate camp life, *intimate Shepperton life.* Perimeter fence, young Jim. Perimeter fence, old Jim, dying man. Pelican.

Shanghai death and trauma, *Shepperton death and trauma.* Martinis. *Johnnie Walker.* American Buick, *Ford Zephyr 6 and Ford Granada.* Boulevards of the French Concession, plane trees. The Ramblas of Barcelona, bull fights, drained river deltas and dried–up river beds. American culture. *Never "rubbish", never "petrol", always "garbage" and "gasoline."*

Fay Ballard, 3 May 2014. Leeds Conference.

© KONINKLIJKE BRILL NV, LEIDEN, 2016 | DOI 10.1163/9789004313866_003

CHAPTER 1

J.G. Ballard and the Drowned World of Shanghai

Graham Matthews

Abstract

J.G. Ballard's *The Drowned World* (1962) presents a panorama of department stores and skyscrapers emerging out of swamplands that evokes the landscape of Shanghai where Ballard lived until he was sixteen. Drawing on historical representations of China in the 1930s and 1940s this chapter reveals the ways in which Ballard incorporated elements of his childhood experience of China into the fictional landscape of *The Drowned World*. Writings about China by Elizabeth Enders, Carl Crow, C.F. Gordon Cumming, Liu Eh, Ruth Hsu and others are compared to Ballard's novel. By investigating the influence of the Shanghai landscape on Ballard's portrait of the submerged London in *The Drowned World*, this chapter indicates the ways in which space and memory influence the fashioning of imaginative truth.

Keywords

J.G. Ballard – *The Drowned World* – Shanghai – China – London – UK – memory – imagination – truth – history – natural disaster – landscape

Ostensibly set in London, *The Drowned World* (1962) presents a panorama of department stores and apartments emerging out of swamplands that evokes the landscape of Shanghai in the 1930s and 1940s where Ballard lived until he was sixteen. Ballard recalls post-war Shanghai as a place filled with abandoned buildings, empty swimming pools and collapsed irrigation systems. This is reflected in the novel by descriptions of the Ritz that are reminiscent of the Peace Hotel on the Bund and by repeated references to bamboo groves, lush vegetation, huge rivers, canals, and flooded paddy fields. Just as various characters in the novel steadily devolve into primordial forms, *The Drowned World* reaches back in time to Ballard's own "archaeopsychic" past and to the formation of his creative imagination. Due in part to the commercial success of his semi-autobiographical novel *Empire of the Sun* (1984) critical attention has typically focused on Ballard's internment in Lunghua Camp, which is often presented as informing his fiction's recurring theme of barely suppressed psychopathy and violence lurking under the surface of civilization. However this is to neglect the vast array of overlapping and competing texts, discourses, ideologies and images that surrounded the nascent author as he grew up in a city that juxta-poses East and West, land and sea, commerce and artistry, wealth and poverty, technology and tradition. As contemporary author Will Self notes, "the Bal-lardian sensibility surely has its crucible just as much in the pre-War Shanghai through which the child Ballard was either ferried in a chauffeur-driven car, or else travelled alone on reckless cycle rides" ("*Crash*: Homage to J.G. Ballard").

In this essay I explore the ways in which space and memory informed Ballard's writing by developing links between the landscape of *The Drowned World* and the advertisements, newspaper articles, stories, rhymes, travelogues, essays, and memoirs that surrounded Ballard as he grew up in Shanghai in the 1930s. My argument does not simply trace the sources for Ballard's works but seeks instead to show how the novel challenges conventional understanding of the text as a unified object, presenting it as a temporary convergence of mul-tiple, overlapping, and competing texts and citations. By stepping beyond the limits of the novel and into the social text of Shanghai in the 1930s and 1940s, memory and by extension the self, I show it to be simultaneously individual and collective, internal and external, subjective and societal.

In a 1975 interview with James Goddard and David Pringle, Ballard discuss-es the impact that the landscape of Shanghai had on his formative years and the sharp contrast between the vibrancy of the Far East and dour post-war England: "It was a very interesting zone psychologically, and it obviously had a big influence – as did the semi-tropical nature of the place: lush vegetation, a totally waterlogged world, huge rivers, canals, paddies, great sheets of water ev-erywhere" (82). By contrast, the English landscape in 1946 is described as pro-vincial, timeworn, and dull: "England was a place that was totally exhausted. The war had drained everything. It seemed very small, and rather narrow men-tally, and the physical landscape of England was so old" (Goddard and Pringle 86). Not only does *The Drowned World* superimpose the semi-tropical land-scape of Ballard's past on to the post-war devastation of his present, the text explicitly comments on the relationship between memory, space, and society.

In 1984, Ballard rejected on moral grounds the notion of a reflexive, self-conscious fiction that explicitly acknowledges the inseparability of author and text: "I regard that whole postmodernist notion as a tiresome cul-de-sac [and] accept that an imaginative writer, like a figurative painter, takes for granted perspective, illusionist space, the unlimited depth of the picture plane" ("Interviews: The Art of Fiction"). Pointing instead to the power of dreams, myths, and legends, Ballard argues that the work of fiction is always already a work of illusion which, in the hands of a skillful writer or storyteller, is able to elicit suspension of disbelief. Ballard maintains that the power of the invented world is found in its ability to re-direct "that old-fashioned imaginative leap," which is routinely imposed upon everyday reality and as such is inextricably linked to the formation and cohesion of communities and civilizations. In this respect his fiction anticipates the work of Benedict Anderson and deals directly with the processes of working mythologies. Because his work is guided by the notion that narratives and unconscious impulses buffer our engagement with reality, Ballard also incorporates elements of "invisible literature" from the world around him: "there are more elements of collage than might meet the eye at first glance. A large amount of documentary material finds its way into my fiction" ("Interviews: The Art of Fiction").

In this respect Ballard's fiction speaks to the concerns of Julia Kristeva who, in *Desire in Language* (1980), argues that the text is both productive and redistributive: "In the space of a given text, several utterances, taken from other texts, intersect and neutralize one another" (36). For Kristeva meaning is never encountered in isolation but mediated by codes produced through a complex network of texts. In common usage the term "intertextuality" has come to stand as a by-word for allusion, devoid of the precision of that term. However as her original formulation indicates, with the collapse of distinct generic categories following the rise of the novel, meaning is increasingly determined in relation to a general text, in other words, through the surrounding culture: "any text is constructed as a mosaic of quotations; any text is the absorption and transformation of another" (66). I would argue that *The Drowned World* anticipates such a reading through the use of water as a symbol alternately of the collective unconscious, of the social (or general) text, and of cultural memory. As the scientist Kerans knowingly states, "perhaps these sunken lagoons simply remind me of the drowned world of my uterine childhood" (*DW* 28). The water is representative of the memories that we do not remember as our own, which in Ballard's fiction are typically projected on to the external landscape in the form of unconscious desires. Kerans possesses the uncanny ability to comment not only on his thoughts and reactions to events but on his unconscious motives as well. In a manner that parallels Kristeva's formulation of the text as a mosaic of quotations, Kerans increasingly struggles to regard himself a self-evident, autonomous individual and instead comes to accept the notion that he is a node in a complex network of intersecting memories and desires.

Ballard's novel has attracted a varied set of critical responses that typically link the highly evocative depictions of place with Kerans' journey into inner space. Peter Brigg, in *J.G. Ballard* (1985), suggests that the submerged city of London symbolises the transitory nature of civilization in the face of nature and notes Kerans' peculiar self-awareness as a detached "scientific" observer and simultaneously as the principal actor in the novel. In *The Angle Between Two Walls* (1997) Roger Luckhurst acknowledges Ballard's use of Jungian archetypes

but reads the novel as primarily an existential allegory. Reflecting on its trans-
position of Dali's iconic imagery, he comments that characters' actions are not
only directed by the landscape but related to a variety of indeterminate frames
and allusions "as if it were possible that Ballard's texts are generated as 'commentaries' or re-narrations of other, only half-discerned texts" (54). In a mirror
of the present study Patrick McCarthy identifies many allusions to the Western
canon, which often suggest ironic parallels between Ballard's fiction and the
work of writers such as William Golding, H.G. Wells, John Donne, and Daniel
Defoe (302–310). Andrzej Gasiorek reads the novel as concerned with questions of identity but focuses on Ballard's scepticism towards the validity of the
scientific worldview in the face of large-scale environmental changes and by
extension, its inability to engage with the innermost recesses of the psyche. He
positions the aquatic realm as an ambiguous site of regression and freedom:
"The lure of the water is associated with threat and succour in equal measure.
Immersion in the lagoons may gesture towards the safety of the womb, but it
is also a passage into the domain of the lizards" (36). For Gasiorek, Kerans un-
dergoes a complete paradigm shift that reorients him away from the remnants
of a superseded civilization but also may not lead him anywhere. Meanwhile,
in *The Psychological Fictions of J.G. Ballard* (2011) Samuel Francis offers a Jungian reading of the novel and questions its problematic attitude towards race.
He notes that despite the validity of Jungian interpretations of Ballard's work,
they are not especially pure and that Ballard also incorporates Freudian concepts within his work. I would suggest that Ballard's simultaneous incorpora-
tion of Freudian, Jungian, existential, and scientific frameworks indicates both
their status and their insufficiency as legitimizing worldviews. Ballard paro-
dies Freud's belief in phylogenetic memory by humorously locating repressed
primordial memories in the spinal column, a point reinforced by Strangman's
subtle mimicry of Kerans' speech patterns and erection of a giant banner over
the lagoon which mockingly reads: "TIME ZONE" (*DW* 97). Perhaps the most
revealing contribution to understanding the novel's emphasis on place comes
from Sebastian Groes who, in an essay that interrogates the role of London
in Ballard's creative imagination, argues that for Ballard the city signifies "the
central discourse of imperial signification" (85). In this respect *The Drowned
World* is reminiscent of Conrad's anti-imperial fiction. It is surprising then
to learn that Ballard claimed not to have actually read Conrad until the early
1970s.[1] Both writers were steeped in colonial discourse before becoming disillu-
sioned with the systems of exploitation and greed that powered the repressive
imperial state. Consequently their fiction appears similar because they draw

---

1   See Jörg Krichbaum and Rein Zondergeld, "It Would Be a Mistake to Write About the Future"
    (*EM* 101) and Patrick McCarthy, "Allusions in Ballard's *The Drowned World*" (*EM* 306).

on a similar array of cultural texts in which London appears as an absent presence against which other cultures are measured.

Three distinct worldviews are presented in the novel: civilization, barbarity, and the primordial, which correspond to Freud's triadic psychic structure of ego, superego, and id respectively. The civilized world is represented by Briggs and is a world of science, observation and measurement, military discipline and order. Following Briggs' departure, barbarity is brought back into the world through the figure of Strangman who is representative of the paternal superego and swiftly instigates a regime of taboo, violence, cruelty, and a perverse morality. Finally Hardman is the representative of the primordial, or the id, who initially escapes from the confines of the military base and ventures into the untamed jungles before finally being blinded by the sun. The contrast between civilization and the primordial is presented as an internal conflict when Kerans steals a compass with no conscious motive of his own:

> Caging the compass, he rotated it towards himself, without realising it sank into a momentary reverie in which his entire consciousness became focused on the serpentine terminal touched by the pointer, on the confused, uncertain but curiously potent image summed up by the concept 'South,' with all its dormant magic and mesmeric power, diffusing outwards from the brass bowl held in his hands like the heady vapours of some spectral grail.
>
> *DW* 46

The annulus has been rotated a full 180 degrees so that the compass points south into the jungles and encroaching flood waters rather than north to the remnants of civilization. The reference to the "spectral grail" alludes to T.S. Eliot's notes to *The Waste Land* and thereby self-consciously presents the signifier "South" as a mysterious, inscrutable Other to Western civilization. For Ballard, "South" primarily signified Shanghai as the Other to Western civilisation and the producer of confused, uncertain but curiously potent images. This notion is reflected in Elizabeth Enders' travelogue *Swinging Lanterns* (1924) in which China is initially presented as a vast, grey, and unknowable land that is resistant to language and description:

> In my school days, China had meant the most difficult part of my geography, with unspeakable names for provinces, and just one river which I could remember – the Yangtze-kiang. Now, in spite of numerous yellow-covered books on the subject and a few brief travelogues, it seemed ever beyond my imagination – as though a great gray curtain were baffling my vision. (3)

According to this narrative China represents an amorphous grey area that is resistant to descriptive prose in ways that parallel the unknowable primordial jungles of *The Drowned World*; this notion is reinforced by Hardman's loss of sight. The overlaying of Shanghai on to the streets of London mirrors Ballard's own sense of inhabiting two distinct worlds at the same time. This sentiment was echoed by Ann Bridge's novel *Peking Picnic* (1932), which opens with the gnomic statement that although the body cannot be in China and Oxfordshire simultaneously it can "travel rapidly between the one place and the other, while the mind or the heart persists obstinately in lingering where the body is not, or in leaping ahead to the place whither the body is bound" (9). Written following her experience in China between the years of 1925 and 1927, she portrays travel as a dislocating experience that opens existential questions of identity and belonging. In *The Drowned World,* Kerans is torn between the world of rationality, order, and science and the encroaching world of irrationality, chaos, and superstition, which exist both as external and as internal spaces. Both Bridge and Ballard record a separation of mind and body as memories of China flood across the English landscape. This suggests that memories, rather than being contained units within the individual, bleed into and are encoded in physical spaces.

Shanghai means literally on the sea and whereas modern-day images of Shanghai are typically of the Pudong skyline, which signals China's financial growth, images from the 1930s and 1940s foreground the Yangtze river, which signals trade and transportation. The newspaperman and businessman Carl Crow in *Foreign Devils in the Flowery Kingdom* (1940) comments that the site, chosen by the Chinese as part of the Treaty of Nanking in 1842, was originally picked out to encourage the Westerners to leave: "The site was a mud flat. The foreshore was flooded with every high tide; the hinterland was covered with mosquito-infested rice fields" (178). On his arrival into Shanghai, the prolific travel writer C.F. Gordon Cumming comments that he found "small attraction in the hideous river and dead-level shores" (2), which he contrasts with the tall and "handsome" houses that had been erected along the banks. He notes that it is all "a very recent alluvial deposit – formed by the ceaseless accumulation of mud washed down by the Great River and its tributaries" (2). Following a trip to China as foreign correspondent for the *Manchester Guardian* in 1927, Arthur Ransome, the author of *Swallows and Amazons* (1930), finds similarities between the flat country and the Norfolk wetlands and whilst riding upstream to Nanking wryly notes that the "foreshore was heavily groined to protect it against the river, which, judging by its colour, is steadily carrying China out to sea" (81). Travellers such as George Smith recorded this phenomenon as early as 1847. He notes that the surrounding country was one continued flat "intersected by numerous little rivers and canals, which effectively drain the soil" (137). This landscape mirrors that of *The Drowned World* in which we learn that U.N. military units use the lagoon systems as avenues of transit "but even these were now being clogged with silt and then submerged" (*DW* 19) while Riggs reveals that in ten years' time "the bigger buildings will have been smothered under the silt" (*DW* 17). The repeated references to silt levels inform the "scientific" section of the novel in which Ballard details a series of gigantic geophysical upheavals in a manner that anticipates the impact of global warming. However, this passage actually minimizes the significance of the rise in global temperatures and the melting of the ice caps and emphasizes instead the dramatically rising silt levels that cause massive deltas to form at the mouths of rivers, "extending coastlines and damming up the oceans," completely altering "the shape and contours of the continents," whilst the cities of Europe are "inundated by the silt carried southwards by the expanding rivers" (*DW* 22). When Hardman escapes from the station, the chase sequence takes place on silt-flats described alternately as "the fetid contents of some latter-day Cloaca Maxima" (*DW* 53) and as "like the backs of yellow sperm whales" (58). The emphasis on silt and cloaca speaks to the broader social text of Shanghai, a city both born from and threatened by the ever-shifting relationship between land, sea, and the river. Ballard's representation of geophysical change is further informed by Chinese perspectives in his use of the simile of a "discarded crown overgrown by wild orchids" (*DW* 21) to describe the abandoned cities, invoking a West–East relation in juxtaposing the Western symbol of monarchical rule with the Chinese symbol of elegance and beauty. This image is thematically linked to the different characters. For "civilized" men like Briggs, the rising water is a threat; for Strangman it is an opportunity for personal gain; whilst for Hardman, and eventually Kerans, it is an alluring yet threatening alternative form of being.

Curiously, in an interview with Travis Elborough, Ballard recalls that Shanghai was struck by floods on an annual basis: "when the winter snows on the Himalayas began to melt and sweep down the Yangtze, there were these huge floods and much of Shanghai was a couple of feet underwater" (3). Although Shanghai did experience flooding, the account provided here is unlikely and the reasoning is highly speculative; instead the comment is indicative of what Ballard considered, in conversation with Cartano and Jakubowski, to be the distinction between the "truth of the imagination" and "prosaic truth" (215). For Ballard the affective impact of any particular scenario is far more significant than the literal record since it is through fiction that one can touch on the obsessions, fantasies, myths, and dreams that flow through society. In the 1980s he repeatedly expressed the notion that the traditional roles of fiction and reality had been reversed by the media landscape, which externalizes the private dreams and fantasies of the individual in a manner comparable to living within an enormous novel. However, *The Drowned World* suggests that long before the development of mass media communications the individual imagination was always already rendered manifest in the form of myths and legends, the Jungian collective unconscious, or the Kristevan social text. When Ballard refers to the "dragon-green, serpent-haunted sea" (*DW* 57), he is referencing the flood narratives that constituted the "truth of the imagination" for many people in China. Verne Dyson, a former Professor of English at Kwang Hua University, gathered together many of China's diverse myths, legends, traditions, and stories in *Forgotten Tales of Ancient China* (1927). Most of the rivers in China are the site of myths and entire families and dynasties often had their fate tied to that of the river. For instance numerous stories are told about the attempt to capture and bind Shui-mu Niang-niang, or the Old Mother of the Waters, who inundated various townships almost every year and carried water buckets with the capacity to flood all of China. There are stories of the engineering works carried out on the Hwai Water that date back over the course of four thousand years. The founding of the Xia dynasty, the first dynasty in Chinese history, is itself linked to floods. Following military defeat at the hands of a noble queen, the chief of the tribes attempted in desperation to end his life and that of his enemies by beating his head against the cane of the Heavenly Bamboo:

> By his mad battering he at last succeeded in knocking down the towering trunk of the tree, and as he did so its top tore great rents in the canopy of the sky, through which poured great floods of water, inundating the whole earth and drowning all the inhabitants except the victorious Queen and her soldiers.
>
> DYSON 225

Since the queen possessed divine status, she was immune to the ravages of the floodwaters and was able to repair the tears in the heavens. In 263 BC Hwang Hien was appointed governor of the region now known as Shanghai for defining the course of the Shen Kiang river. Deepening its channel allowed ships with heavy tonnage to sail upstream and bring wealth and prosperity to the nascent state. It is now known as the Hwang Pu River in his honour. The care of rivers was pivotal to the plot of the satirical *Tramp Doctor's Travelogue* written by the scholar and poet Liu Eh and translated in 1939. It depicts China under the old Manchu regime, devastated and desolated by flood and famines, misruled and misgoverned by a class of conceited bureaucrats. As this brief survey indicates, within Chinese culture floods signify as aspects of divine judgment, as well as opportunities for political power and feats of engineering. Although a scientific rationale is given for the floods in *The Drowned World*, the jungles are imbued with a phantasmagoric and mythical power that exerts an irresistible hold over the inhabitants of the lagoon while political power in the novel is closely tied to Strangman's dramatic feat of engineering when he reveals the submerged London beneath the waters.

The stories, myths and legends that surround China's rivers and waterways indicate that they were not simply physical features of the landscape but were deeply embedded in the cultural imaginary as potent sources of fear and inspiration. As a child Ballard would have been surrounded by legends and tales about floods that later became a prominent feature of children's rhymes and stories. The American author Ruth Hsü lived in Nanking in the 1930s and collected rhymes from immigrants from across the country, including Shanghai. Her collection suggests that such memories are not simply individual but are in a constant process of becoming within a continuously evolving community. In the foreword John Ferguson recalls, "Some family that settled in this city brought this ditty with them and its catching rimes stuck in the memory of neighbours till it became really a local possession" (iv). According to Hsü old folk rhymes were still being used in Chinese schools in the 1930s as a light-hearted foil to the formal education predicated on rote learning and gradual understanding of the Confucian texts. The rhymes constituted an alternative to this severely regimented system and gave expression to the popular attitudes and wisdom of the common people. They are typically humorous in the face of oppressive circumstances such as famine, drought, war and floods, and gently mock customs, traditions and social archetypes. "When Will It Rain?" typifies this approach:

> When the gay clouds southward float,
> Put out the large family boat;
> When the gay clouds northward roam,
> The flood waters will soon come;
> When the gay clouds eastward go,
> A strong wind will surely blow;
> When the gay clouds westward keep,
> The Goddess Wong puts on her rain-cape. (30)

To some extent this rhyme mirrors the myriad weather prophecies such as "Rain," "The Winds" and "March Winds" contained in the English *Mother Goose* but clearly differs in its open acceptance of the power of nature over all human (and godly) endeavour. Traces of the rhyme's combination of fatalism and frivolity can be witnessed in Kerans' and Hardman's insouciant attitude towards climate change. The emphasis on rivers and floods also appears in English-language children's literature such as Eleanor Lattimore's *Little Pear* published in 1931. This text concerns the adventures of a five-year-old Chinese boy, who at the novel's climax falls into the water, is rescued by a family on a houseboat, and consequently experiences a moral epiphany. This novel reaffirms the centrality of the river to Chinese culture whilst establishing a clear division between life on the river and life on the land. Lattimore dwells on traditions and superstitions such as good luck charms and the reason why boats have eyes painted on them in a manner that purports to teach American children about China but instead reductively emphasizes the universality of childhood experiences. The text glosses over social inequalities but nevertheless the class divisions related to life on the river and life on land are clearly discernable.

Rather than address the severe social inequalities in Shanghai, Western accounts typically comment on the prevalence of disease and establish a causal relation with the climate. An advert for a medicine called Aspro in the *North-China Daily News* entitled "Fagged Out Through Heat" states: "Nothing is more enervating than humidity, excessive heat and sunglare, which seriously saps the human vitality." Ballard similarly equates the climate with enervation: "several times within the past month the generator had failed to respond immediately to the thermostat, and the temperature was well into the nineties, probably responsible for Beatrice's lethargy and ennui" (*DW* 50). Ballard's tongue-in-check hypothesis that the reformed climate and landscape is causing individuals to regress to their primordial origins in the Triassic period may also double as a critical response to stereotypes about the Oriental character as "indolent" and "lethargic." The ineffectual nature of the scientific observatory, which has not collected any useful data and is powerless in the face of continuing solar activity, implicitly challenges the notion that Western science was needed to combat the backward superstitions of the East. Many Western texts on China attempt to characterize the collision between East and West in terms of a difference between rational science and foolish superstition yet often inadvertently reveal some degree of self-criticism and doubt. *Doctors East Doctors West* (1946) charts Edward Hume's efforts to establish a medical centre as part of the Yale-in-China initiative (Yali) in Changsha, Hunan province. The book turns on the dynamic between the supposedly self-evident superiority of "modern" Western medicine and the ill-defined and ultimately indeterminate "wisdom" to be found in the ancient traditions of the Orient. In this respect it speaks to Ballard's portrayal of man's reliance on scientific knowledge in the face of the alien landscape. The first in-patient at Hume's hospital is soon diagnosed with double lobar pneumonia and, despite the "vivid, ineffaceable guide" (59) of Western medicine, his condition steadily worsens and he becomes critical. Hume is forced to acknowledge the apprehensions of the mother, his coolie T'ou Sz-fu, and the broader social context. As Sz-fu states:

> Yes, sir, you are very wise. But I know what the people in our street are say-
> ing. I know their thoughts. You don't understand, sir. Suppose he should
> die in the hospital. All your work of these past weeks would be undone
> [...] please take no chances now. I beg you to send the boy home before
> there is an accident. (61)

Hume realizes that he must acquiesce to the wishes of the mother and the community by sending his critically ill patient home. If the boy had died in the ward, news of the death would have spread throughout Hunan province and it would have set back the progress of Western medicine in China by many years. As his language tutor Liu later clarifies, the reason lies in the "superstition" that at the point of death "the body is kept in the home awaiting the return of the soul. It is very serious for death to occur away from home, for the wandering soul may not find the body" (62). Hume treats this explanation as an issue to be overcome rather than considering the myth's importance for sustaining familial bonds and by extension the wider community.

The preoccupation with science as the chief distinguishing factor between China and the West continues in *The Lady and the Panda* (1938), which details Ruth Harkness' long and demanding journey through China to the border of Tibet in order to capture a rare mammal that had never previously been held in captivity. She returns to Shanghai in order to make the return flight to America and it is at this stage that she reflects on the significance of the panda in Chinese culture and considers the ethics of removing the creature from its natural habitat. However these concerns are only raised in order that they may be immediately dispelled. She meets with an "influential person" in China's government who offers the young fashion designer and socialite complete reassurance:

> I was doing the right thing, the influential person said. I had avoided
> publicity, had stirred up no antagonism that might result from the public
> being given to understand that I was taking a rare and valuable animal
> out of China. Why shouldn't I take Su Lin [the panda] to America, where
> there were facilities to raise her to adulthood, and where science was
> equipped to make use of the knowledge to be gained from a live Panda?
> China had no such facilities. (194)

Harkness removes a nine-week-old living symbol of national pride under the justification that Western science would make better use of the animal. Furthermore this retroactive justification occurs after she admits that the unorthodox exhibition had been conducted without the knowledge or permission of the Academia Sinica because "I wasn't a scientist and knew that I would have been refused" (193). From our twenty-first century vantage point, it is difficult not to read such an account as a form of cultural colonialism, retroactively legitimized under the auspices of scientific investigation. As these descriptions show, the division between the "scientific" West and the "superstitious" East was an integral part of the social text of Shanghai and frequently used to justify Western presence in China. In response to anti-imperialist criticism Harley MacNair declared in an article entitled "Some Asian Views of White Culture":

> In the present age the West has developed scientific thought and scientific method; it discourages slipshod thinking and muddle-headedness and indirectness. This a great part of the East lacks, and this it can and should learn from the West. (85)

MacNair presents science as a means of increasing the productivity of the country through the installation of labour-saving devices, the construction of famine-prevention measures and irrigation systems, and the dissemination of new agricultural methods. For MacNair, scientific discourse functions as a synecdoche for Western imperialism and is presented as indisputably superior regardless of socio-cultural specificities or ethical concerns. In this light Ballard's sceptical portrayal of scientific research in *The Drowned World* doubles as an anti-imperialist critique. The recording instruments of the testing station are undoubtedly ineffectual for the process of coming to terms with the radically new environment, for bringing order and method to the remnants of society, or for engaging with the hidden depths of the psyche. As Riggs reflects, "all the work we've done has been a total waste – as I have always maintained, incidentally" (*DW* 15). Instead the testing station reflects Ballard's concern that scientific discourse can be used or misused as a tool of administration, instrumental reason, and control.

The myriad overlapping and competing discourses that comprise the social text of Shanghai play a major role in framing Ballard's portrayal of regression from civilization to nature, from outer to inner space, from rationality, logic, and order to instinct, fluidity, and myth. Rather than focusing on Ballard's wartime experiences, my purpose has been to shed some light on a hitherto concealed aspect of Ballard's literary imagination. The cultural texts presented above suggest that Ballard's oft-remarked disillusionment while standing on the deck of the ship at Southampton docks arose out of a belief that was inculcated within him at an early age in the technological and moral superiority of the West. By figuratively flooding the imperial centre in *The Drowned World*, Ballard confronted Western notions of science and progress with the inescapable and alien power of the environment and, by extension, the depths of the human mind. I hope to have demonstrated that this dynamic was already playing out in the discursive construction of Shanghai in cultural texts that emphasized the power and immensity of nature and dwelt on the mythological status of water and floods, and also in texts that portrayed science and reason as a justification for economic inequality, cultural colonization, and scientific endeavour. At the conclusion to *Empire of the Sun*, on the eve of his journey to Britain, a strange country he had never visited before, Jim remarks that "only part of his mind would leave Shanghai. The rest would remain there forever, returning on the tide" (*ES* 351). As a fictional cipher for Ballard himself, Jim's premonition is particularly apt, for when Ballard created the London landscape of tomorrow, the drowned world of Shanghai surfaced from the past.

Works Cited

Anderson, Benedict. *Imagined Communities: Reflections on the Origin and Spread of Nationalism*. London: Verso, 2006.

Ballard, J.G. and Thomas Frick. "Interviews: The Art of Fiction." *Paris Review* 94 (1984). Web. 17 September 2015. <http://www.theparisreview.org/interviews/2929/the-art-of-fiction-no-85-j-g-ballard>.

Blakiston, Thomas. *Five Months on the Yang-tze; with a Narrative of the Exploration of its Upper Waters, and Notices of the Present Rebellions in China*. London: John Murray, 1862.

Bridge, Ann. *Peking Picnic*. Harmondsworth: Penguin, 1938.

Brigg, Peter. *J.G. Ballard*. Mercer Island, WA: Starmont House, 1985.

Cartano, Tony and Maxim Jakubowski. "The Past Tense of J.G. Ballard." Translated by Dan O'Hara (*EM* 211–33).

Crow, Carl. *Foreign Devils in the Flowery Kingdom*. Harper and Brothers, 1940.

Cumming, C.F. Gordon. *Wanderings in China: Volume II*. Edinburgh: William Blackwood and Sons, 1936.

Dyson, Verne. *Forgotten Tales of Ancient China*. Shanghai: The Commercial Press, 1927.

Elborough, Travis. "Reality is a Stage Set." *The Drowned World*. London: Fourth Estate, 2012. Pp. 2–7.

Enders, Elizabeth. *Swinging Lanterns*. New York: D. Appleton and Company, 1924.

Francis, Samuel. *The Psychological Fictions of J.G. Ballard*. London: Bloomsbury, 2011.

Gasiorek, Andrzej. *J.G. Ballard*. Manchester: Manchester University Press, 2005.

Goddard, James and David Pringle. *J.G. Ballard: The First Twenty Years*. Hayes: Bran's Head, 1976.

Groes, Sebastian. "From Shanghai to Shepperton: Crises of Representation in J.G. Ballard's Londons." *J.G. Ballard: Visions and Revisions*. Edited by Jeannette Baxter. London: Continuum, 2008. 78–93.

Harkness, Ruth. *The Lady and the Panda: An Adventure*. London: Nicholson and Watson, 1938.

Hsü, Ruth. *Chinese Children's Rhymes*. Shanghai: The Commercial Press, 1935.

Hume, Edward. *Doctors East Doctors West: An American Physician's Life in China*. New York: Norton, 1946.

Krichbaum, Jörg and Rein Zondergeld. "It Would Be a Mistake to Write About the Future." Translated by Dan O'Hara. *EM* 99–105.

Kristeva, Julia. *Desire in Language: A Semiotic Approach to Literature and Art*. Translated by Thomas Gora, Alice Jardine, Leon Roudiez. New York: Columbia University Press, 1980.

Lattimore, Eleanor. *Little Pear: The Story of a Little Chinese Boy*. New York: Harcourt, Brace and Company, 1931.

Liu, Eh. *Tramp Doctor's Travelogue*. Trans. Lin Yi Chin and Ko Te-Shun. Shanghai: The Commercial Press, 1939.

Luckhurst, Roger. *"The Angle Between Two Walls": The Fiction of J.G. Ballard*. Liverpool: Liverpool University Press, 1997.

MacNair, Harley. *China's New Nationalism and Other Essays*. Shanghai: The Commercial Press, 1926.

"Aspro is Invaluable on Hot Trying Days." *The North-China Daily News*. 11th July 1937.

McCarthy, Patrick. "Allusions in Ballard's *The Drowned World*." *Science Fiction Studies*. 24.2 (1997): 302–310.

Ransome, Arthur. "Up the Yangtze to Hankow." *Readings in Modern Journalistic Prose*. Ed. Lin Yutang. Shanghai: The Commercial Press, 1931.

Self, Will. "*Crash*: Homage to J.G. Ballard." *Crash Exhibition*. London: Gagosian Gallery, 2010. Web. Accessed 17 September 2015. <http://will-self.com/2010/04/19/crash-homage-to-jg-ballard/>.

Smith, George. *A Narrative of an Exploratory Visit to Each of the Consular Cities of China and to the Islands of Hong Kong and Chusan, in Behalf of the Church Missionary Society in the Years 1844, 1845, 1846*. London: Seeley, Burnside, & Seeley, 1847.

CHAPTER 2

Aeolian Harps in the Desert: Romanticism and *Vermilion Sands*

Thomas Knowles

Abstract

This chapter explores the legacy of Romanticism in J.G. Ballard's *Vermilion Sands*, and the presence of that collection in *The Atrocity Exhibition*'s "The Summer Cannibals." Drawing upon the aesthetic theory of Wordsworth's "Preface" to *Lyrical Ballads*, as well as the literary criticism of M.H. Abrams, it reads the sonic sculptures and singing statues of *Vermilion Sands* as warped reincarnations of the Romantic Aeolian harp, played upon by the wind and by the lamia-like muses that figure in each story.

Keywords

J.G. Ballard – *Vermilion Sands* – Romanticism – Aesthetics – Sublime – the death of affect – imagination

J.G. Ballard describes *Vermilion Sands* (1971) variously as "an exotic suburb of [his] mind"; "between Arizona and Ipanema Beach"; and as part of the "3,000 mile-long linear city that stretches from Gibraltar to Glyfada Beach" (*vs* 7). The resorts of Vermilion Sands, Red Beach and Lagoon West are at once otherworldly and familiar, evoking Mediterranean sun-drenched villas and apartment complexes as well as the dreamscapes of Surrealism and, I would suggest, the Romanticism of English poetry. Supernatural elements of the landscape take the form of jewelled insects, sand rays, singing statues and sonic sculptures, as well as sentient architecture and clothing, and lamia-like faded screen actresses and heiresses. Surrounded by sand seas, multi-coloured sand reefs and fused lakes, the natural world is as exhausted as its beach-fatigued human residents. The denizens and visitors of *Vermilion Sands* are affectless, bored, capricious and always on the lookout for new ways to stimulate their decadent imaginations. Yet in his descriptions of this future-past world Ballard evokes a lyrical, sometimes decadent, poetry.

The *Vermilion Sands* collection bookends Ballard's career just as *The Atrocity Exhibition* (1970) stands at its centre. Published individually between 1956 and 1970, these short stories include Ballard's first professionally published fiction, "Prima Belladonna" (1956), whilst "Say Goodbye to the Wind" (1970) takes us up to the publication of *The Atrocity Exhibition*. Their resonance can be clearly detected in the "Summer Cannibals" chapter of *The Atrocity Exhibition* and also extend into the final quartet of Ballard's novels, becoming infused in the specified nowheres of *Cocaine Nights* (1996) and *Super-Cannes* (2000). Ballard, in an interview with Will Self, suggested that authors do not necessarily write their works in the correct order, and that *Vermilion Sands* ought to have been his last book,

> I have often thought that writers don't necessarily write their books in their real order. *Empire of the Sun* may well be my first novel, which I just happened to write when I was fifty-four. It may well be that *Vermilion Sands* is my last book.
>
> EM 314

Vermilion Sands, then, is a presence before, after and throughout the universe of Ballard's writing, a location suggestive of the aesthetic of the sublime, which this chapter will trace through the perpetuation and disavowal of Romanticism in both *Vermilion Sands* and *The Atrocity Exhibition*.

The nine short stories that make up *Vermilion Sands* have been read in Jungian terms as an externalization of the warring elements of the psyche in the self's quest for individuation.[1] References to Surrealist art works, painters and textual effects abound too.[2] However, the texts also support a reading which sees them as experiments in the calibration of the imaginative faculty which mediates between mind and world, and therefore as epistemological tales that both perpetuate and critique the Romantic drive to synthesize the dichotomous relationship between subject and object. This is an explicitly Romantic concern, and the oscillations in Ballard between the dejection of the "death of affect" (or "beach fatigue" as it is referred to in these stories) and the engorged imagination that would remake the world in an aesthetic revolution, hinge

---

1   See for example William M. Schuyler, 'The Portrait of the Artist as a Jung Man: Love, Death and Art in J.G. Ballard's Vermilion Sands' (1993), in *New York Review of Science Fiction* no. 57 (May 1993): 8–11, and no. 58 (June 1993): 14–19.

2   See Jeannette Baxter's *J.G. Ballard's Surrealist Imagination: Spectacular Authorship*. London: Ashgate, 2010. Although *Vermilion Sands* itself is not covered in detail, many of Baxter's insightful readings are equally applicable to these stories.

upon that subjective/objective divide which featured so prominently in the poetry and critical debates of the Romantic era. Ballard's use of such Romantic tropes and of lyrical language forms, I would claim, is part of a nexus of textual resonances, which include psychoanalysis and Surrealism, and allow Ballard to create responses in the reader that often run entirely counter to the plotted events of a text, thus achieving a perpetual ambivalence, or a studied ambiguity.[3] Ballard seems to confirm the existence of this triumvirate of influences upon his work in answer to a question from Christopher Bigsby for the *Writers in Conversation* series,

> Yes, I think I am a romantic. I feel my links are not with any writers or school of writing but really with the surrealists. I am an old-fashioned surrealist, probably the last of them. I think there is a strong strain of romanticism running through surrealism. It is romanticism making a strange mixed marriage with psychoanalysis. It is the informed waking dream. But it is still a dream in some ways and I think there are dream-like and romantic elements running through my fiction. I am glad they are there. (79)[4]

In this essay I offer a Romantic reading of the sonic sculptures and singing statues that populate the decadent beach resorts and the sand sea, and of the wind that plays upon them. I also address related Romantic themes and tropes which occur in these and in Ballard's other fictions, as part of a wider understanding of J.G. Ballard as an imaginative author who engages with and critiques Romantic concerns in the twentieth and twenty-first centuries. My focus is on "The Cloud Sculptures of Coral D" and other stories from the collection which I attempt to link with the "Summer Cannibals" section of *The Atrocity Exhibition*. For my definitions of Romanticism I draw upon the literary and aesthetic theory of William Wordsworth's "Preface" to the 1802 edition of *Lyrical Ballads*, as well as upon the Romantic theory and criticism of M.H. Abrams, whose work is roughly contemporaneous with the first fifteen years of Ballard's writing. Particular attention is given to Abrams'

---

3   For an account of the psychoanalytic and psychological components in Ballard, rather than psychoanalytic readings of his works, see Samuel Francis's *The Psychological Fictions of J.G. Ballard* (London: Bloomsbury, 2013).

4   I came across this quotation by asking Mike Bonsall's "Ballard-Bot," "Are you a Romantic?" The bot searches a database of interviews and opinion pieces for relevant answers to your questions. <http://demo.vhost.pandorabots.com/pandora/talk?botid=f6e046f76e347da1>.

The Mirror and the Lamp (1953), "The Correspondent Breeze: A Romantic Metaphor" (1960), and *Natural Supernaturalism* (1973).

Romantic Aesthetics

The Aeolian harp or wind harp is a wooden, stringed instrument which is played upon by the wind. In the late eighteenth century it became a symbol for creativity and the beauty of the natural world, especially for the authors and poets we now call Romantic. Coleridge's "Dejection: An Ode" (1802) and his "The Eolian Harp" (1795), provide the best known examples of the symbolic appearance of the instrument in poetry, and the psychical journey that the ode describes is also a movement that can be traced in the stories of *Vermilion Sands*. Abrams outlines it thus,

> The rising wind [...] serves as the vehicle for a complex subjective event: the return to a sense of community after isolation, the renewal of life and emotional vigour after apathy and spiritual torpor, and an outburst of creative inspiration following a period of sterility.
>
> "Correspondent Breeze" 113–114

That the singing statues and sonic sculptures of *Vermilion Sands* are metaphorical devices of a comparable significance in the landscapes of Ballard's fiction may be immediately acknowledged by the reader of Ballard. In particular there seems to be an invitation to hone in on the phrase "spiritual torpor," which Abrams borrows from Wordsworth's "Preface," and to bring it into dialogue with the Ballardian concept of the "death of affect." In his introduction to the 1975 French edition of *Crash*, Ballard defines "the death of affect" as "the most terrifying casualty of the [twentieth] century," a "demise of feeling and emotion" which accompanies a capacity to take pleasure in pain, mutilation and the pursuit of "our own psychopathology as a game" (*R/S JGB* 96).

Two components of Wordsworth's thought in his "Preface" may be of particular interest when considering Ballard's portrayal of a "death of affect," and his aestheticizing of the "technological landscape" (*C* viii). These are, firstly, the poet's insistence upon the need for poetry and poets to cleanse the perception of city dwellers, who are benighted by an "almost savage torpor" and a "degrading thirst after outrageous stimulation" (Wordsworth 599); and, secondly, his prophecy of the place of the poet in a world transformed by technology, which was only beginning to beckon from the margins at the dawn of the nineteenth century:

If the labours of Men of Science should ever create any material revolution, direct or indirect, in our condition, and in the impressions that we habitually receive, the Poet will sleep then no more than at present, but he will be ready to follow the steps of the Man of Science, not only in those general indirect effects, but he will be at his side, carrying sensation into the midst of the objects of Science itself. (606–607)

It is clear enough that Ballard's writing makes good on the prophecy concerning the role of the writer in relation to the man of science. More significant still may be the lasting resonance of Wordsworth's intention to lift city dwellers out of their "savage torpor," in Ballard's descriptions of "beach fatigue" and the "death of affect." "Beach fatigue" is peculiar to Vermilion Sands and its neighbouring resorts and is described variously as "lethargy"; "irreversible boredom and inertia"; "a limbo of endless sunbathing, dark glasses and afternoon terraces"; and "heavy dreamless sleep" with insidiously numbed senses, blunting despair and hope (*VS* 19, 51, 147, 157, 175).[5] Compared to the cold and flattened psychopathology of the denizens of Ballard's later cityscapes, this "beach fatigue" seems a relatively benign version of the "death of affect," perhaps representing "the most terrifying casualty of the [twentieth] century" on holiday (*R/S JGB* 96). Both early and later versions involve something like Wordsworth's "thirst after outrageous stimulation," and the outrageous lengths to which the characters of these stories will go in order to feel something is a part of the driving force behind the psychopathological behaviour witnessed in the *Vermilion Sands* stories, in *The Atrocity Exhibition* and *Crash*.

In these later fictions Ballard's aesthetic invokes the familiar landscapes of urban modernity in a process of defamiliarization. Motorway overpasses, access roads, empty car parks, high-rise buildings and shopping centres, which have been rendered invisible through overfamiliarity, are revealed anew by an apocalyptic gaze. Ballard's fiction thus cleanses the perception of the city dweller and allows us to see these objects aesthetically transformed into the beautiful, the sublime, the terrifying and the horrific, and in such a way that they rekindle dormant affect. A major component of Wordsworth's aesthetics, particularly as evidenced in *Lyrical Ballads* (Wordsworth 597), is the attempt to imbue the ordinary and everyday with a sheen of unfamiliarity, to find the supernatural in the natural so that the subject perceives anew and with childlike wonder, the approach that M.H. Abrams defines as his "natural supernaturalism." If we see the urban landscape as somehow natural to the

---

5   Five of the nine *Vermilion Sands* stories refer to "beach fatigue" by name, but the sense of malaise permeates all of them (*VS* 19, 51, 147, 157,175).

modern city dweller in this sense, then we can admit Ballard's reinvigoration of the affecting qualities of our environment as another kind of "natural supernaturalism." Abrams, in *Natural Supernaturalism*, reads Wordsworth's famous Gondo ravine passage, in Book VI of *The Prelude*, as the momentary synthesis of the "ineluctable contrarieties" of the beautiful and the sublime in human existence (Abrams *Natural Supernaturalism* 106–107). A comparable tendency is discernible in Ballard, when the depiction of sublime terror is lavished with lyrical prose, rendering the terrifying and abhorrent somehow beautiful.

Meanwhile, in the stories of *Vermilion Sands*, Ballard's "natural supernaturalism" is given a complementary Coleridgean inversion, one in which a fantastical or supernatural landscape of haunted mariners roaming the desert seas can be rendered somehow natural. In this supernatural landscape myth meets modernity and modernity meets the transformative imagination, turns into solipsistic nightmare, and is rescued by the hope of creative renewal. Ballard, in a seemingly Romantic gesture, has brought the landscape, or nature, back into the equation.

Whilst the "beach fatigue" of *Vermilion Sands*, with all of its passionless levelling of experience, might seem an unlikely place to look for Romantic echoes, Ballard's depiction of this casualty of the twentieth century might be read as a brutal diagnosis and a nihilistic, satirical celebration of modernity and postmodernity and their ills. Such a bleak portrayal also suggests that things might be otherwise and perhaps that they ought to be, in the tradition of William Blake's depiction of industrialization's "dark Satanic mills" (161), or in the critique of over-stimulated city life in Wordsworth's "Preface" to *Lyrical Ballads*. Such a tradition is in keeping with Ballard's studied ambiguity and ambivalence, since in the stories discussed below he seems at once to be denigrating this affectless realm whilst celebrating its limitless potentiality. There is decadence in the lifestyles of the denizens of Vermilion Sands, Red Beach and Ballard's other beach resorts, shown in their limitless freedom to pursue their own psychopathologies, and in their sense of sensory exhaustion. On a Romantic plane, the very ephemerality and diffuseness of the resort lends it the quality of a Romantic fragment or dream, briefly gesturing towards a sublimely vast whole before melting into isolated remnants at the season's end.

The Wind in Romanticism and in *Vermilion Sands*

The mode of creative reinvigoration in these nine stories calls upon the Romantic metaphors of personified wind and the Aeolian harp in the form of singing statues and sonic sculptures. In Romanticism the wind is a literary and artistic master metaphor for change, creative inspiration and the capricious aspects of the natural world. It is worth noting that the wind was also Ballard's earliest metaphor for catastrophic change in his novels, the first of which was *The Wind from Nowhere* (1962). This ephemeral but demonstrably real force can carry a sailor home across the wide sea, but may just as likely stir up a storm and wreck ships upon rocks, or drive them out into the frozen wastes as in Coleridge's "The Rime of the Ancient Mariner." The air, whether moved by human intervention or by natural forces, is not just a literal aspect of the landscape but a metaphor for change in the poet's mind. Coleridge's "Dejection: An Ode" is a classic example of the wind viewed as inspiration, of the poetry of Romanticism as being "thoroughly ventilated" as Abrams puts it (113). The poet/speaker's "dull pain" of dejection, which is the occasion of the poem, and Ballard's condition of "beach fatigue" – "The beach fatigue from which I suffered numbed the senses insidiously, blunting despair and hope alike" (*vs* 175) – are surprisingly conversant:

> A grief without a pang, void, dark and drear,
> A stifled, drowsy, unimpassioned grief,
> Which finds no natural outlet, no relief. (Coleridge *Major Works* 114)

Moreover, the way in which the wind acts upon the speaker and the "Eolian lute" in the poem, corresponds very closely with the plotted events of the first story in *Vermilion Sands*, "The Cloud Sculptors of Coral D" (1967). In Coleridge's poem, the speaker's state of alienation and creative stagnation is at first plagued by, but then finally transcended and alleviated by, the ministrations of the wind upon the Aeolian Harp, his metaphor for the natural world's working upon the mind of the speaker. The discordant notes the storm plucks from the harp allow the speaker to feel and inhabit the state of dejection and this in turn provokes those dormant powers of creativity into describing his melancholy state. Thus primed, when the rising storm of the wind plucks from the harp an alarming succession of notes ending in a cacophonous crescendo, the speaker's imagination is fired-up, producing lines of lyrical intensity. The poem, however, ends on an ambivalent note. The state of dejection to some extent returns, but with the knowledge gained from the frightening but invigorating intervention of the natural world, and the concomitant waxing of the imaginative power. Abrams sees in this condition both the reinvigorating potential of the natural, phenomenal world, and the deliberate transfer of its power into the subjective realm of the speaker's imagination (Abrams "Correspondent Breeze" 117). Through this movement, the speaker takes command of that which he had been subject to, so that a future stimulation of the imagination will be possible through a reflection on this internal world.

Such a reconfiguration of the phenomenal world into a source of internal visionary potential seems to have intriguing parallels with Ballard's "The Cloud Sculptors" and the other stories of *Vermilion Sands*. Major Parker, the narrator of "The Cloud Sculptors," is a retired pilot with a leg injury which prevents him from flying, an ailment that is immediately suggestive of wounded or dormant imaginative capacity, flight (according to T.E. Hulme) being another Romantic master metaphor.[6] Driving into the desert, Parker stops to observe the coral towers on the road to Lagoon West. There he hears the music of some sonic statues which have "run to seed" (*vs* 11), and follows it to an abandoned workshop where he builds kites and gliders which hang tethered above him "in the afternoon air like amiable ciphers" (*vs* 12). As in Coleridge, change is heralded here by the wind: "A sudden gale rose over the crest of Coral D" and in its wake appear Petit-Manuel and Nolan, later to be joined by Van Eyck (*vs* 12). These are the pilots who will do what Parker cannot and take to the skies in order to sculpt the clouds. The artist and pilot Nolan tightens the helixes of the sculptures by the workshop to make them sound more tuneful. This one event can be read as a microcosm for Ballard's engagement with Romanticism and for the similitude between the sonic sculptures of *Vermilion Sands* and Aeolian harps. The sonic sculpture is discovered abandoned and in disrepair in the desert, a dessicated hulk which no longer produces a tuneful sound. The glider-mechanic, though, an artist himself, is able to adjust its helixes and make it harmonious with its surroundings once more. We can understand this moment as a Ballardian discovery of Romantic sentiment and feeling, amongst the "pseudoevents, science and pornography" of modernity (*R/S JGB* 96). By updating its symbols and through a marriage of modern technology and inward shamanism, Ballard resurrects the ghost of this movement as a potential force for personal and social revolution. Put another way, in Andrzej Gasiorek's terms, Ballard "draws imaginatively on the resources of Romanticism" in order to "re-mythologize the past, present and near future" (48).

Coleridge's poem follows a process, which Abrams describes as "the renewal of life and emotional vigour after apathy and spiritual torpor, and an outburst of creative inspiration following a period of sterility" (115). The early pages of "The Cloud Sculptors" follow this pattern closely enough. The transience of cloud sculptures aligns them with the ephemerality of music, their dependence upon the wind with that of the wind harp, and with the fickle nature of

---

6   T.E. Hume claimed, for example, "You might say if you wished that the whole romantic attitude seems to crystalize in verse around metaphors of flight" (*Speculations* 120).

inspiration. The troupe of sculptors craft gorgeous, vanishing displays out of their windborne medium,

> Lifted on the shoulders of the air above the crown of Coral D, we would carve seahorses and unicorns, the portraits of presidents and film stars, lizards and exotic birds. As the crowd watched from their cars, a cool rain would fall on to the dusty roofs, weeping from the sculptured clouds as they sailed across the desert floor towards the sun.
>
> *VS* 11

The passage evokes the exoticism and wistful longing of a Romantic fragment, a lyricism which resonates throughout the collection. Much like the music of the wind harp, the sculptors' creations are fleeting, momentary, and they are soon destroyed by the very wind that was instrumental in their production. In Coleridge's ode the wind rises to a storm pitch that frightens and invigorates the speaker, prompting the poem's most impassioned lines. Leonora Chanel, the retired movie star and patron of the cloud sculptors, seems to be able to exert some control over the wind that bears them on its shoulders, driving them to ever-greater heights of aerial acrobatics and sculpting prowess. Her patronage, however, like that of the muses of old, requires sacrifice, and she claims the lives of two of the gliders before Nolan drives the storm against her, after which he vanishes. The cloud sculptors are inspired to produce their "strangest portraits" by this troubled muse of the story, whose images "carved in the whirlwind, were to weep their storm-rain upon the corpses of their sculptors" (*VS* 11). Through their self-sacrifice in pursuit of their art, the cloud sculptors fit the type of the Romantic hero, expiring for the sake of art and for want of recognition by their fickle muse. The forces that the wind-summoned imagination conjure-up prove fatal in this instance, but there remains the possibility of creative endeavour; Nolan may have survived and there are rumours of his exploits in other resorts and towns (*VS* 30). The narrator is content to listen to the sculptures at night with Leonora's secretary. Calm is restored and knowledge of the imaginative faculty has been gained, and its return, heralded by the wind, is anticipated:

> In the evenings Beatrice and I sit among the sonic statues, listening to their voices as the fair-weather clouds rise above Coral D, waiting for a man in a dark-winged glider, perhaps painted like candy now, who will come in on the wind and carve for us images of seahorses and unicorns, dwarfs and jewels and children's faces.
>
> *VS* 30

This pattern of torpor, followed by a reinvigoration of the imagination, and a final wistful reminiscence, looking forward to further bouts of tumult, is repeated in the subsequent eight stories of the collection. Configurations, artistic pursuits, professions and locations are moved about like pieces on a chess board, and outcomes vary slightly. All of the nine stories are reminiscences of times gone by, and each story features a muse figure. There are nine muses corresponding to those of antiquity, and each sets off a chain of resonances with classical and Romantic literature.

The women of *Vermilion Sands* are the destabilizing but creatively invigorating force that blows through each story, fulfilling the role of the wind in Coleridge's ode and playing upon the "strings" of the sonic statues and singing sculptures. In his treatment of Leonora Chanel, and the other exotic female figures of the stories, Ballard seems to reproduce the gendered stereotypes of Romantic aesthetics. If we see in "The Cloud Sculptors" the dramatization of the artist Nolan's attempt to experience and master the sublime in the shape of the storm, then Leonora Chanel's broken body manifests the rejected feminine that has been considered a by-product of the masculine sublime,

> Leonora's body lay among the broken tables near the band stand, half-wrapped in a bleeding canvas. Her face was as bruised now as the storm-cloud Manuel had tried to carve.
> *VS* 29

In the confusion of Leonora's bleeding body with the canvas of one of her many portraits, the climax of the story suggests a moral judgement on the glamorous and vain woman's extreme narcissism. Leonora's secretary, Beatrice, says as much, but hints at something more, "carving one's portrait in the sky out of sun and air – some people might say that smacked of vanity, or even worse sins" (*VS* 21). Peter Shaw in his account of the sublime suggests that,

> Where women appear in [canonical] Romantic poetry, therefore, it is either as the discarded material excess of sublime empowerment, a principle of opposition to be resisted, or as the nurturing, beneficial foil to fantasies of narcissistic reintegration. (105)

When Leonora first appears, the womanizing Van Eyck heralds her thus, "look at what arrives – my apocalypse [...]" (*VS* 16), and the fascination with which she is viewed is maintained from then on, the descriptions of her clothing and persona recalling the mythological figure of the lamia, the paintings of Delvaux, and the perceived dangers of feminine excess, "with the diamonds fixed around her eyes she reminded me of some archaic priestess. Beneath the contour jewellery her breasts lay like eager snakes" (*vs* 23). An apocalypse is also a revelation, though, and through Leonora's excess there seems to be a glimpse of the numinous, fraught with the inherent dangers of dissolution. Leonora attempts the masculine sublime in her wish to dominate the storm and remake it in her own image, but she also gestures towards the material excess that, according to Shaw, threatened to overrun Burke's definition of the beautiful, destabilizing its distinction from the sublime (Shaw 59–61). Perhaps Leonora's supposed crime, then, was that of a female attempting to assume the mantle of the sublime. The narrator's preference for the "pretty and agreeable" Beatrice over her mistress, a "pale chimera with jewelled eyes" (*vs* 17), offers another instance of this masculine opposition of the sublime and the beautiful, according to which the domain of the feminine is confined to the small, pleasing and knowable.

Complex gendered tropes that seem to echo those of Romanticism are also present in the other stories of *Vermilion Sands*, including "The Singing Statues" (1962), where the statues of the title sing of its tragic heroine. Chopped up and abandoned in the desert to rust, they take root again and come uncannily back to life, continuing to sing in a pale parody of their former resonance, a discordant echo. They are ugly, decaying, traumatized almost, and yet Ballard's prose wrings from them a melancholic beauty. In this passage the statues sing of Lunora Goalen, another of *Vermilion Sands*' apocalyptic muses,

> No one tends the sculptures now and most of them have gone to seed, but on an impulse I cut away a helix and carried it back to my villa, planting it in the quartz bed below the balcony. All night it sang to me, telling me of Lunora and the strange music she played to herself […]
>
> *vs* 75

Their music is described as being "Like a forgotten lover, whispering over a dead harp" (*vs* 89), a corpse music borne on a sepulchral wind, evoking a decadent sensibility. This seems once again to concern the ability to create meaningful or resonant art in the beach-fatigued world of *Vermilion Sands*. The artistic productions of the twentieth century display the wounds of atrocities past and future, doubly haunted by the ghosts of the past and the spectre of a future used up. There is something cruel and disquieting about the part-living, part-sculpted forms, the malleability of their bodies and their refusal to stay dead. In them something approaches an extreme metaphor for the immanence of the phenomenal world that Abrams calls "natural supernaturalism," and Ballard characteristically combines disgust and wonder in these tortured harps.

In "The Screen Game" (1963), the narrator returns to a seemingly abandoned summer house each day to play the "screen game," and echoes of sonic statues drift across the sand dunes on the wind to him, stirring memories of Emerelda Garland and her jewelled insects. The framing sections at the beginning and end of the story imbue the tale with a melancholy longing. Rearranging what remains of the painted screens, in an echo of the game that had been part of a film in which Emerelda was to star, creates a sense of compulsive repetition and a kind of mourning. The rekindled imagination that had spawned the painted screens, the retelling of the Orpheus myth, and the coaxing of the starlet out of the summer house to wander amongst the film crew are now distant memories. The statues that had lined the road have fallen silent and the air of the place is sepulchral, and we see something like the state of beach fatigue in the long creative interregnum that the film production had woken the narrator and his friends from. However, in the act of reminiscence and memorialization, a wistful lyricism infuses the language and thus imagination is reborn even as its loss is lamented:

> All over the deserted summer-house the low refrain was taken up by the statues, echoing through the empty galleries and across the moonlit terraces, carried away to the mouths of the sand reefs, the last dark music of the painted night.
>
> VS 73

In describing Coleridge's ode Abrams sees a comparable process at work:

> By the agency of the windstorm it describes, the poem turns out to contradict its own premises; the poet's spirit awakes to violent life, even as he laments his inner death, achieves expression in the despair at being cut off from outlet of expression, and demonstrates the power of the imagination in the process of memorializing its failure.
>
> ABRAMS "Correspondent Breeze" 115

This speaks to a Ballard who, in the very act of describing the dearth of all that might be called Romantic, uses lyrical language and the symbols of the imagination: the deep self, the wind, flight and birds, jewelled objects and pale, deathly women of decadent desire.

In some traditions it is Orpheus who is credited with having invented the lyre, or with having increased the number of its strings to nine to reflect the nine muses (March 551–554). In the layering of myths upon myths in the landscape of "The Screen Game," the myth of Orpheus and his death and mourning are also present. Through the singing statues the demise of the film producer, Charles Van Stratten echoes around the landscape that witnessed it, performing an act of mourning of which their human creators seem incapable:

> By some acoustic freak, the dead sculptures along the beach had revived themselves, and once again I heard the faint haunted echoes of Charles Van Stratten's last cry before he was killed by the jewelled insects.
>
> VS 73

For the Romantic poets of nature, Coleridge and particularly Wordsworth, the natural world was a living canvas upon which the history of the individual mind could be projected and read, but technology and the products of science were seen largely as invasive, alienating factors in the estrangement of man from a benevolent nature. Ballard here unsettles this assumption with a rendering of the technologically-perverted singing statues, half of the natural world and half synthetic, as the repositories of affect and emotion which their decadent creators can no longer feel. "Prima Belladonna" (1956) adds another dimension to this inverted anti-Enlightenment strain in its vision of a future in which the human singing voice has been replaced by scientifically-mutated plants. The narrator, Parker, sells singing plants in his shop, above which he and his friends spend most of their time drinking beer and playing "iGo." The plants are maintained by a cocktail of gasses and nutrients, keyed up or down chemically as required and tuned by a monstrous "Khan Arachnid" plant. Much like the poetry-producing machines of "Studio 5, The Stars" (1961), these plants have largely rendered human talent redundant. Jane Cyracylides blows through this sleepy resort like an invigorating wind, firing up long dormant libidos and latent imaginations. Jane's vocals provoke hallucinations, and her singing voice is a sensation with which even the genetically modified plants cannot compete. When she first arrives Jane is compared to a force of nature, a muse, a goddess, perhaps even an incarnation of the imagination itself (VS 32). There are no sonic sculptures in "Prima Belladonna," but along with the singing flowers we might consider Jane Cyracylides as another female muse-like embodiment of the "correspondent breeze" whose capriciousness and ephemerality form part of the allure. Just as the singing statues and sonic sculptures of the other stories are repositories for dormant affect, the singing plants of "Prima Belladonna," and the poetry machines of "Studio 5, the Stars," intervene between humanity and the natural world. Their ambiguous roles include both the suppression of the imaginative faculty and its safeguarding; one might say that the problem provides the material out of which it is to be solved.

"Locus Solus" and *The Atrocity Exhibition*

If *Vermilion Sands* ought to have been Ballard's last book, then perhaps the world that *The Atrocity Exhibition* describes is drawing us ineluctably towards that exhausted future. In some respects the symbolic landscape of the *Vermilion Sands* stories is revisited in "Locus Solus," apparently the setting for "The Summer Cannibals" chapter of *The Atrocity Exhibition*, borrowing, as Ballard indicated, the title of a novel by Raymond Roussel (*AE* 99). In his notes, Ballard sets out its peculiar appeal,

> The curious atmosphere of the Mediterranean beach resorts still awaits its chronicler. One could regard them collectively as a linear city, some 3000 miles long, from Gibraltar to Glyfada beach north of Athens, and 300 yards deep. For three summer months the largest city in the world [...] The usual hierarchies and conventions are absent; in many ways it couldn't be less European, but it works. It has a unique ambience [...] At present it is Europe's Florida, an endless parade of hotels, marinas and apartment houses, haunted by criminals running hash from North Africa, stealing antiquities or on the lam from Scotland Yard.
>
> *AE* 99

The landscape of "The Summer Cannibals" is almost beatific in contrast to the extreme atmosphere of menace, derangement, violence, sexual perversion, degradation and black humour that marks many other chapters of *The Atrocity Exhibition*. The components of Traven's fragmented identity in *The Atrocity Exhibition*, variously Travis, Traven, Talbot, Tallis, Trabert, Talbert and Travers, seem to anneal on this endless beach and fade into a dreamlike erasure, as Ballard puts it in his marginal gloss: "This is Traven again [...] but a Traven devoid of those larger concerns that preoccupy him elsewhere in the book" (*AE* 100–101). If "beach fatigue" was described above as a version of the "death of affect," it may be that these non-place resorts represent its true home and birthplace,

> Could it ever become Europe's California? Perhaps, but the peculiar geometry of those identical apartment houses seems to defuse the millenarian spirit. Living there, one is aware of the exact volumes of these generally white apartments and hotel rooms. After the sombre light of northern Europe, they seem to focus an intense self-consciousness on the occupants. Sex becomes stylised, relationships more oblique.
>
> *AE* 100

Yet whilst the leisure location of Locus Solus resembles the Romanticism of *Vermilion Sands* the dominant experience and context of *The Atrocity Exhibition* suggests a more extreme response to modernity that would require exploration in terms of a more extreme Romantic aesthetic of discordant contraries. Most of the *Vermilion Sands* stories had been written by the time Ballard embarked on his project of writing "condensed novels" that would ultimately become *The Atrocity Exhibition*. In an update on his new fictional work for the October 1966 edition of *New Worlds*, Ballard categorized his new model as analytic rather than synthetic, "the analytic function of this new fiction should not be overlooked. Most fiction is synthetic in method – as Freud remarked, rightly I feel, a sure sign of immaturity" (Ballard "Notes from Nowhere" 151). If the *Vermilion Sands* stories can be said to have celebrated the combinatory powers of the imagination, then in *The Atrocity Exhibition* we witness the pulling apart of contrarieties, suspended in dialectical opposition. This opposition, however, does not necessarily produce a stasis, but can be seen as productive according to another model associated with Romanticism: the energetic Blakean tensions of texts such as *The Marriage of Heaven and Hell*, in which dynamism is produced through the clashing of contraries. The power to pull apart the overlapping fictions of what Ballard calls the "media landscape" (*AE* 37), however extreme, might in this Blakean sense suggest a possibility that the components become available once more for recombination. It is here that the full sublimity of the human imagination is realized in all of its terrifying glory, able, not only to symbolically connect disparate concepts, but to pull apart the seemingly inseparable and re-make them in new and unexpected ways.

In the *Vermilion Sands* stories the protagonists remained largely passive, happy to await their apocalypse in whatever form it happened to manifest itself. In contrast the T-characters of *The Atrocity Exhibition* are determined to induce their apocalypse through a wilful refashioning of the media landscape in which they are trapped. There are multiple and contradictory drives in *The Atrocity Exhibition* towards reconciliation with the alienating environment of modernity, and the personal and historical traumas of the twentieth century. These include a drive towards affectless abstraction in which the soft curves of the human form intersect with the "motion sculpture" (*AE* 108) of motorway access ramps and overpasses, the chromium detailing and instrument binnacle mouldings of the motorcar. Here, human bodies, speech acts and gestures are figured as moduli, which can be fitted into grand forms, whether geometric, architectural, mythological or elemental. The goal of this drive is dissolution, forgetfulness, amniotic return, and easeful death. "The Summer Cannibals" chapter perhaps sees the apotheosis of this mode with its unnamed central character and the falling away of the wider concerns of the rest of the novel, concentrating instead on abstract sexual acts and listless *dérives* around the dried up river beds and sand dunes that surround the white apartment buildings of Locus Solus. Allied to this movement in the novel is the finding of equivalence in personal acts, gestures and appearance with the topography of the media landscape; the merging of the media landscape with the internal landscape so that the exploration of a terrain is simultaneously the traversing of a film star's body, or the inside of a character's skull or spinal levels.

The almost opposite movement seems aimed at piercing the smooth and placid surfaces of modernity and the media landscape, reinvigorating memory and keeping alive creativity and imagination through extreme measures. This movement is obsessed with the creation and reopening of wounds, both those of the human body and psychological and historical traumas. The wounded human body insists on the biological, the animal and the feeling. It opens up the victim to the world and to others. The rough surfaces of wounds, of bodily imperfections and of environmental decay, resists the homogenization and dissolution of the first movement, insisting on the real and determining to puncture the mediatized agglomeration of fictions that occlude the vision. The fetishization and aesthetic display of wounds is decadent, but it seems a decadence which paradoxically aims at reawakening dormant affect. Pain, violence and the restaging of historical catastrophes and disasters aim at keeping these wounds fresh, awakening memory and desire. In this movement it is assumed that we all carry radiation burns from Hiroshima and Nagasaki, are burdened by the unassuaged guilt of the Holocaust, and are obliquely responsible for the deaths of Marilyn Monroe, James Dean, John Fitzgerald Kennedy and the Apollo astronauts.

These complex movements are highly ambiguous, each regularly overlapping the other and partaking of opposite aesthetics and effects. The restaging of historical disasters, for instance, as well as working to keep the decaying memory of these disasters alive, works to subsume personal trauma into the wider form of historical disaster. The loss of one's spouse becomes another of the "myriad deaths of the cosmos" (*CSS1* 263), and the opening of a wound can paradoxically enact the circularity of both closure and repetition. The pitting and marking of the canvas of the human skin becomes a part of the erosive forces of time that have decayed both the natural and built environments. The repositioning of the human body as a Hans Bellmer[7] doll, manoeuvrable into abstract and cryptic poses and shapes, can very easily slide into a psychopathic dissociation from pain inflicted upon bodies, and even a fascist intolerance

---

7   Hans Bellmer (1902–1975) was a German sculptor, photographer, painter and writer, famous for his unsettling doll sculptures, which evoke E.T.A. Hoffmann's "The Sandman" and transgressive sexuality. See, for instance, *Die Puppe* (1934) and *The Doll* (1937–8).

for the stain of life upon the clean and smooth geometric eternity. In this way the first movement leads to the second movement through the wounding of bodies which awakens affect, if not in the central characters themselves then in the reader. In *The Atrocity Exhibition*, then, the cold and emotionless realms of modernity provide the raw material for the reawakening of dormant affect.

Works Cited

Abrams, M.H. *Natural Supernaturalism: Tradition and Revolution in Romantic Litera-ture.* London: W.W. Norton and Company, 1973.

Abrams, M.H. "The Correspondent Breeze: A Romantic Metaphor." *The Kenyon Review* 19:1 (Winter, 1957): 113–130. Web. 13 June 2015.

Ballard, J.G. "Notes from Nowhere." *New Worlds* 50:167 (October 1966): 147–151.

Baxter, Jeannette. *J.G. Ballard's Surrealist Imagination: Spectacular Authorship.* London: Ashgate, 2010.

Bigsby, Christopher. *Writers in Conversation: Volume 1.* London: Pen & Inc Press, 2000.

Blake, William. *William Blake: Selected Poetry.* Edited by Michael Mason. Oxford: Oxford University Press, 2008.

Bonsall, Mike. "Ballard-Bot." Web. 17 September 2015.

Coleridge, Samuel Taylor. *Samuel Taylor Coleridge: The Major Works.* Edited by H.J. Jackson. Oxford: Oxford University Press, 2008.

Francis, Samuel. *The Psychological Fictions of J.G. Ballard.* London: Bloomsbury, 2013.

Gasiorek, Andrzej. *J.G. Ballard.* Manchester: Manchester University Press, 2005.

Hulme, T.E. "Romanticism and Classicism." *Speculations.* London: Routledge, 2000. 111–140.

March, Jenny. *The Penguin Book of Classical Myths.* London: Penguin, 2008.

Schuyler, William M. "The Portrait of the Artist as a Jung Man: Love, Death and Art in J.G. Ballard's Vermilion Sands." *New York Review of Science Fiction* 57 (May 1993): 8–11, and 58 (June 1993): 14–19.

Shaw, Peter. *The Sublime.* London: Routledge, 2006.

Wordsworth, William. "'Preface' to *Lyrical Ballads*" [1802]. In *William Wordsworth: The Major Works.* Edited by Stephen Gill. Oxford: Oxford University Press, 2008. 599.

CHAPTER 3

Zones of Non-time: Residues of Iconic Events in Ballard's Fiction

Catherine McKenna

Abstract

When he died in 2009, J.G. Ballard left a private library collection in his estate. The items held in this collection form a landscape of influence and inspiration for Ballard's work, particularly the writing from the creative period which resulted in texts such as "The Terminal Beach," *Crash, Concrete Island* and *The Atrocity Exhibition*. The collection contains many items which fit the description Ballard coined of "invisible literature," and this essay examines two such items in that collection which deal with the cultural landscape of the twentieth century: the iconic events of the advent of the atomic bomb and the assassination of John F. Kennedy. The representation of the physical and psychological impact of these traumatic events in Ballard's work is explored, along with a discussion of Ballard's interrogation of rigid narratives of historical discourse.

Keywords

J.G. Ballard – invisible literature – Pacific Islands – assassination – John F. Kennedy – nuclear age – Ballard's personal library

When J.G. Ballard died in 2009, he left a collection of manuscripts and a private library collection in his home. The manuscript collection was donated to the British Library in 2010, leaving his personal library in the private hands of his estate, where it remains. This collection was catalogued from 2011 to 2012, and represents a relatively small collection of 565 items taken largely from Ballard's study, where he wrote. The main genres represented within the collection are Art, Literature, History and Cultural Studies, Science, Film and Television and Architecture, with a large collection of maps also present.[1]

---

1 Ballard's library collection and its contents remain the copyright of the J.G. Ballard Estate. The items in this essay are discussed with the very kind permission of the estate.

When examining this library collection, the items which are most striking are those which can be grouped under a title coined by Ballard himself, that of "invisible literature." In many interviews and non-fiction writing throughout his career, Ballard spoke of his interest in invisible literature, which he defined as "scientific journals, technical manuals, pharmaceutical company brochures, think-tank internal documents, PR company position papers" (Fraser 94) and "the internal memoranda of TV company planning departments, sex manuals, U.S. government reports, medical textbooks" (*R/S JGB* 156). Ballard's personal library collection contains many items which fit this description, in particular U.S. government reports, scientific journals, technical manuals and medical textbooks. This material is most clearly relevant to the period surrounding the production of texts such as "The Terminal Beach" (1964), *The Atrocity Exhibition* (1970), *Crash* (1973), and *Concrete Island* (1974), as well as "surgical fictions" such as "Princess Margaret's Facelift" (1970), which were eventually included in editions of *The Atrocity Exhibition*. This chapter will explore two examples of Ballard's invisible literature: *Operation Crossroads* (1946), the official pictorial record of the 1946 United States atom bomb tests on the Pacific Island of Bikini, and *The Official Warren Commission Report on the Assassination of President John F. Kennedy* (1964), a U.S. Government report produced in the aftermath of the shooting of JFK.

In approaching research on any library collection, the mind is inevitably drawn to theories of collecting, curating, archiving and knowledge management or control. Whilst all books can been seen as archival in a sense, as "material substrate[s]" in Derrida's terms (8), what is striking about the invisible literature in Ballard's collection is that it includes items for which concepts of archiving, historical narrative and knowledge control are central. The two items on which this essay will focus are official government reports, concerned with the management of information surrounding iconic moments in history, and with the creation and control of the historical narrative of these events, constructing the landscape of collective memory. As Helen Freshwater has observed,

> [The] interaction of the state, writing, and the archive not only demonstrates the importance of textual traces for the construction of identity and collective national memory, it also indicates the state's methods of maintaining control of its subjects. (733)

Indeed, Ballard's interest in invisible literature stems from a concern with the accessibility of knowledge and information; the manner in which knowledge is controlled and the creation of historical narratives. As Ballard asserts in relation to another example of invisible literature, *Crash Injuries*, in an interview from 1982, "access to a book like that is not easy. For one thing, you're never told about the *existence* of the book [...]" (*R/S JGB* 10). Ballard's interest thus comes from a desire to access information that is routinely kept from the majority of the public. Here, I will explore how the experimental nature of Ballard's texts disrupts and transforms the persistently coherent narrative of events presented by these official publications, and how the obsessive desire of his protagonists to revisit the sites of trauma and re-enact iconic moments "sustains the challenge to official notions of endings and beginnings which is staged obsessively throughout Ballard's fictions" (Baxter 159).

Ballard is a writer often associated with non-places: the car parks, airports and motorway underpasses of modern landscapes. Yet there is another interesting aspect of space in Ballard's work, in the many stories and novels that deal with spaces and places which have historical significance and how this history leaves a residue on the landscape, a haunting which seems to fascinate him. In particular, *The Atrocity Exhibition* and a significant precursor to that text, the short story "The Terminal Beach," demonstrate an interest in the the historical events of atomic bomb testing in the Pacific and the assassination of John F. Kennedy: Dealey Plaza in Dallas, Texas. In these two texts, the protagonists are drawn to the sites of these iconic events, as if the landscapes of such historical moments retain an aura of what happened there.

These sites are forever transformed by these moments, both physically and figuratively, becoming archival sites of cultural memory. Ballard's texts explore the evidence that remains of these traumatic moments in history on the physical and cultural landscape, evoking the ruined architecture of Pacific test sites and the geometry of the site of Kennedy's assassination, as well as the psychological impact of these significant moments on the popular psyche through the protagonists of "The Terminal Beach" and *The Atrocity Exhibition*.

Ballard's texts emphasize the nature of these locations as archival sites, or material substrates upon which archival traces are etched, through his repeated descriptions of elements of the landscape as ciphers and cryptic alphabets. As Roger Luckhurst observes, the "incidence of codes, forms of writing, manifesting themselves 'unreadably' within the landscape" (68). This trope is evident in both "The Terminal Beach" and *The Atrocity Exhibition*: "The landscape of the island was covered by strange ciphers" (*CSS2* 29); "the tall palm trees leaned into the dim air like the symbols of a cryptic alphabet" (*CCS2* 29); "the slides of exposed spinal levels in Travis's office. They hung on the enamelled walls like the codes of insoluble dreams" (*AE* 1); "overhead wires like some forgotten algebra of the sky" (*AE* 68). These landscapes are imprinted with signs, ciphers, and physical evidence, forming an alternative archive of the trauma that took place there. The island of Bikini, where the Operation Crossroads bomb tests took place, still to this day contains radioactive traces in the soil. Dealey Plaza, where Kennedy was killed, now has a white X marking the spot on the road where the first shot hit, as well as hosting the Sixth Floor Museum, located in the Book Depository Building, where Oswald fired the fatal shots. These landscapes are inscribed with the signs of the events, becoming substrates upon which archival evidence is etched, or in the case of Dealey Plaza, becoming an archive or museum of the event: an atrocity exhibition, even.

Doorways into Another Continuum

Many of Ballard's characters have been drawn by the lure of Pacific Islands containing concrete runways, bunkers, blockhouses and camera towers. Traven in "The Terminal Beach" is drawn to the concrete blockhouses at the centre of Eniwetok island, "a zone devoid of time" (*CSS2* 36). Neil in *Rushing to Paradise* is drawn to the island, Saint-Esprit, because it is, "a nuclear test-site, like Eniwetok and Kwajalein Atoll" (*RP* 26). Melville in "My Dream of Flying to Wake Island" is obsessed with Wake Island, not a nuclear test-site but a coral atoll which served as an air force base during World War II.

As Ballard wrote in his 1990 annotations to the *Atrocity Exhibition*,

> Pacific islands with their silent airstrips among the palm trees, Wake Island above all, have a potent magic for me. The runways that cross these little atolls, now mostly abandoned, seem to represent extreme states of nostalgia and possibility, doorways into another continuum.
>
> *AE* 52

Ballard's interest in these deserted Pacific atolls, whose idyllic beauty has been transformed by the addition of concrete runways and blockhouses, has strong connections to one particular item in his library collection, *Operation Crossroads: The Official Pictorial Record*. This book is a historical record of Operation Crossroads, the atomic bomb tests nicknamed Able and Baker (A and B tests) on the coral atoll of Bikini in the Pacific Ocean, carried out in July 1946. It contains a large amount of photographic evidence of the tests, with images of their preparation and implementation, as well as the explosions themselves.

FIGURE 3.1 *Frame from "Camera Tower Construction Enyu Island – Bikini Atoll, 05/29/1946"*
(Joint Task Force One, The Office of the Historian, 29). [2]

At once an official government publication, a historical document and a pictorial record, *Operation Crossroads* embodies Ballard's fascination with visual
imagery, as well as the representation of iconic cultural events in official governmental narratives. It is a text heavily imbued with official narrative and a
desire to control the story of this historic moment. As such, the government
document is resolutely positive and determined to represent the tests as a non-
aggressive, scientific endeavour. As the introduction to the text makes clear,

---

2   This image, and the majority of the images contained within *Operation Crossroads* are Joint
     Task Force photographs, which are now held at the US National Archives. This particular
     image would appear to be a frame taken from a film reel "CAMERA TOWER CONSTRUC-
     TION ENYU ISLAND – BIKINI ATOLL, 05/29/1946," from the series "Moving Images Relating
     to Military Activities, compiled ca. 1947–1980." (NAIL Control Number: NWDNM(m) – 428-
     NPC-18195). *Operation Crossroads* 29.

The purpose of these tests was to determine the effect of the atom bomb against various types of naval vessels. With the information secured, we can improve our ship design, tactics, and strategy, to minimize our losses in the unfortunate event of war waged with atomic weapons [...] With such a plan, atomic energy can in time become the controlled slave of man's peacetime pursuits.

Joint Task Force One, The Office of the Historian 6

The images contained within this book of camera towers next to palm trees and white sand beaches (See Figure 3.1), are strikingly reminiscent of Ballard's stories, which abound with descriptions of beaches, bunkers and camera towers, "in the night air they passed the shells of concrete towers, blockhouses half buried in rubble..." (*AE* 3); "A disused runway moved through the grass. Partly concealed by the sunlight, the camouflage patterns across the complex of towers and bunkers four hundred yards away revealed half-familiar contours [...]" (*AE* 10); "Each afternoon he left his cell in the abandoned camera bunker among the dunes and walked down into the blocks" (*CSS2* 33). The juxtaposition of the beauty of the coral atolls with the death and destruction associated with the atomic tests, as well as the unnatural harshness of the concrete infrastructure which the tests required, was clearly influential source material for Ballard's work. In *Operation Crossroads*, the landscape of camera towers and test equipment is presented in a very positive manner, with the camera towers themselves described as "lofty grandstand seats" (29). This landscape is transformed in Ballard's text into a ruined space, "disused" and "half buried in rubble." Ballard's text thus comments on the pride expressed in *Operation Crossroads* and calls into question the narrative of the tests and their impact as it is presented in the text.

"The Terminal Beach" is set on Eniwetok, another atoll in the Marshall Islands, which was used by the United States government for bomb testing during the years 1948–1958. The island is described in the text as "zone of non-time" (*CSS2* 33), a sense derived from its association with the advent of nuclear fission, a transformative moment in modern history. Ballard's description of Pacific Islands as "doorways into another continuum" is connected to their role in the testing of atomic bombs and thus their proximity to the possibility of apocalypse. This connects to Ballard's earlier disaster novels, with the catalyst for apocalyptic change in "The Terminal Beach" being the advent of atomic fission. For Ballard, such significant events present extreme states possibility: a way of stepping outside into a zone of non-time. This sense of being out of time is a motivating factor in the compulsion of Traven, the protagonist in the story, to go to Eniwetok. Suffering in the aftermath of the death of his wife and son, Traven's desire to escape to a zone of non-time is his way of dealing with the tragedy, perhaps even in the vain hope of rewriting the past. He reads the deaths of his wife and child as part of the destruction caused by nuclear fission and the new world order haunted by atomic fear:

> Even the death of his wife and six-year-old son in a motor accident seemed only part of this immense synthesis of the historical and psychic zero, the frantic highways where each morning they met their deaths the advance causeways to the global Armageddon.
>
> CSS2 32

Ballard's protagonist struggles to come to terms both with personal and with larger cultural traumas in society. He re-enacts significant historical events, returning to their locations, in an effort to excise personal trauma. The T-character in *The Atrocity Exhibition*, as Webster explains it, also repeatedly re-enacts such events as the JFK assassination and the deaths of the three *Apollo* astronauts, a compulsive remembering, in an effort (amongst countless other motives) to escape the trauma of his own past:

> 'The bomber crashed on landing,' he explained. 'Four members of the crew were killed. He was alive when they got him out, but at one point in the operating theatre his heart and vital functions failed. In a technical sense he was dead for about two minutes. Now, all this time later, it looks as if something is missing, something that vanished during the short period of his death. Perhaps his soul, the capacity to achieve a state of grace. Nathan would call it the ability to accept the phenomenology of the universe, or the fact of your own consciousness. This is Traven's hell. You can see he's trying to build bridges between things – this Kennedy business, for example. He wants to kill Kennedy again, but in a way that makes sense.
>
> AE 50

Here Traven's attempt to "build bridges between things," recalls the protagonist of the earlier story, in his efforts to draw connections between personal tragedy and broader historical events. In "The Terminal Beach" Traven was drawn to the Pacific Island site of death and destruction as a way of excising his own suffering through the mass traumas caused by the bombing of Hiroshima and Nagasaki, and also the countless future deaths to be caused by nuclear weapons. Remembering in order to forget is central to this story, with Traven's "Catechism of Goodbye" being the only thing that provides relief from the overpowering presence of the concrete blocks which dominate the landscape of the island,

> '*Goodbye, Eniwetok*,' he murmured.
> Somewhere there was a flicker of light, as if one of the blocks, like a counter on an abacus, had been plucked away.
> *Goodbye, Los Alamos*. Again, a block seemed to vanish. The corridors around him remained intact, but somewhere in his mind had appeared a small interval of neutral space.
>
>   *CSS2* 45

Yet he remains unwilling or unable to let go of his personal trauma, choosing instead the haunting figures of "his wife and son watching him from the dunes" (*CSS2* 50).

This desire to re-enact moments of cultural trauma in order to make sense of personal trauma, is a trope which appears in several of Ballard's works, such as the semi-autobiographical fiction, *The Kindness of Women* (1991),

> If death had out-stared life, which the world seemed to believe, I could rest my case. In a desperate sense Miriam would be alive again, Kennedy would drive triumphantly through Dealey Plaza, the casualties of the Second World War would rest in their graves [.]
>
>   *KW* 229

Ballard makes connections between the personal trauma of his own wife's death, and wider cultural traumas. He further elaborates this in his autobiography, *Miracles of Life* (2008) where the partly-fictionalised Miriam is now more clearly revealed to be a reference to his wife Mary,

> I was trying to construct an imaginative logic that made sense of Mary's death and would prove that the assassination of President Kennedy and the countless deaths of the Second World War had been worthwhile or even meaningful in some as yet undiscovered way.
>
>   *ML* 207

Ballard's work therefore questions the desire to create definitive accounts of cultural trauma, impeding as this does a greater understanding of the implications of traumatic incidents, both collective and individual. Ballard's texts explore the potential for finding resolution to personal traumas in the larger traumas which have affected twentieth-century cultural life, endeavouring to find meaning in the collective in order to resolve the personal.

The desire of both Traven in "The Terminal Beach" and the T-character in *The Atrocity Exhibition* to reimagine the past is indicative of the significant correlation between these two works. "The Terminal Beach" is a clear pre-cursor to *The Atrocity Exhibition*, with the obsessions of the T-character in *The Atrocity Exhibition* mirroring the obsessions of "The Terminal Beach," with time and Eniwetok: "This strange man, and his obsessions with time, Jackie Kennedy, Oswald and Eniwetok" (*AE* 43). The immense destructive power of the atomic bomb, and the subsequent post-war nuclear age which followed the bombs at Hiroshima and Nagasaki, is a central concern of *The Atrocity Exhibition*. As Andrzej Gasiorek argues, "*The Atrocity Exhibition* is haunted by the implosion of space-time caused by nuclear fission, which destroys vast tracts of space and shatters the lived time of numberless individuals" (65). "The Terminal Beach" is also a stylistic pre-cursor to *The Atrocity Exhibition*, with its short, titled paragraphs, as Luckhurst asserts: "'The Terminal Beach' was the first of Ballard's 'condensed novels,' the stripping down of narrative into sharply defined units of imagistic prose. The text appears in brief, titled 'blocks' of prose" (68). This stylistic trope has a corollary in the invisible literature of Ballard's library collection, as this essay will further explore. *The Atrocity Exhibition* follows on from the obsession with the advent of nuclear fission in "The Terminal Beach" and builds on it to explore the spectrum of popular cultural events of the twentieth century, most significantly the assassination of John F. Kennedy.

The location of the assassination of John F. Kennedy at Dealey Plaza in Dallas, Texas, is a location which holds an abiding interest for Ballard, and is a site returned to throughout *The Atrocity Exhibition*, but also returned to some forty-years after the publication of this text in Ballard's novel *Super-Cannes* (2000): "I tried to imagine Lee Harvey Oswald on his way to the book depository in Dealey Plaza on the morning he shot Kennedy" (*SC* 178); "May 28 was our Dealey Plaza. Like it or not, it's all the history we have" (*SC* 172). The T-character in *The Atrocity Exhibition* is described as being obsessed with Dealey Plaza, the location of Kennedy's death, "the geometry of the plaza exercised a unique fascination upon Talbot's mind" (*AE* 25). Dealey Plaza re-occurs several times in the text, in keeping with Travis's obsession with re-enacting the events of the assassination, for example, "her leg stance, significant indicator of sexual arousal, confirmed all Dr Nathan had anticipated of Trabert's involvement with the events of Dealey Plaza" (*AE* 66); "'This motorcade,' Dr Nathan explained, 'we may interpret as a huge environmental tableau, a mobile psycho-drama which recapitulates the Apollo disaster in terms of both Dealey Plaza and the experimental car crashes examined so obsessively by Nadar" (*AE* 73).

The T-character's mind is constantly drawn back to the location of this trauma, as if an aura of the events which took place there still remains in the geometry of concrete, book depository and overpass. He appears to sense that there is a clue to the meaning of this tragic incident which remains at Dealey Plaza, and by psychologically revisiting the site through his re-enactments, that he can somehow discover the latent meaning in the event, "to kill Kennedy again, but in a way that makes sense" (AE 50).

Ballard's experiments with the transformative possibilities of factual and authoritative texts are explored in *The Atrocity Exhibition* through the use of *The Official Warren Commission Report on the Assassination of John F. Kennedy*. This report was the result of the deliberations of the Warren Commission, formed by Lyndon Johnson two weeks after the assassination to investigate the event. It is both a historical and a scientific text, with detailed examinations of injuries, trajectories and angles, as well as eyewitness statements, and detailed background information on Lee Harvey Oswald. As a historical text, it has been widely criticized and many of its conclusions disputed.[3] As Barbie Zelizer asserts,

> The commission's speedy resolution of the assassination, however, left unanswered some vital questions concerning how and why the murder took place. This was due in part to the time pressures surrounding deliberation, which left large holes on the official record. Questions persisted concerning the reasons for Oswald's involvement, the mechanics of that involvement, and the contradictory eyewitness testimony that suggested the involvement of others.
>
> ZELIZER 106

It is just such ambiguity of interpretation which is appealing for Ballard in his use of the *Warren Commission Report* as an influence in his work, commenting as he did that, "in its way it's remarkable – if it were a novel you'd say it was a

---

3   The House Select Committee on Assassinations, which published its report in 1979, asserted that Oswald likely acted as part of a conspiracy, and that "The Warren Commission failed to investigate adequately the possibility of a conspiracy to assassinate the President" and "The Warren Commission presented the conclusions in its report in a fashion that was too definitive." (4, 5) The Assassinations Records Review Board in 1998 also called into question the conclusions of the Warren Commission, reporting that many high profile figures had doubted the findings of the Commission, "Doubts about the Warren Commission's findings were not restricted to ordinary Americans. Well before 1978, President Johnson, Robert Kennedy, and four of the seven members of the Warren Commission all articulated, if sometimes off the record, some level of skepticism about the Commission's basic findings" (11).

masterpiece. And it may very well *be* a novel, because a lot of its conclusions have been challenged" (*R/SJGB* 10).

The *Warren Commission Report* has a clear stylistic correlation to the form of *The Atrocity Exhibition* with its short paragraphs and headings in bold, "Tolerances of the Human Face" (*AE* 107); "The Skin Area" (*AE* 79); and "The Impact Zone" (*AE* 65). The *Warren Commission Report* is also broken down into sections and sub-sections, often with obscure headings in bold, and Ballard was obviously influenced by this disjointed and fragmented style in his creation of *The Atrocity Exhibition* and "The Terminal Beach." David Punter has written of the style of *The Atrocity Exhibition* that it "is written in separate, headlined paragraphs to resemble brief newspaper articles" (Punter 135). The style of *The Atrocity Exhibition* can indeed be seen as reflective of short newspaper articles, but it also bears a startling resemblance to the style of the invisible literature in Ballard's library, many of which are structured in short paragraphs with sub-headings, which seem quite obscure when taken in isolation. As Ballard himself writes of the *Warren Commission Report*,

> the bizarre chapter titles – 'The Subsequent Bullet That Hit', 'The Curtain Rod Story', 'The Long Bulky Package' – together suggest a type of obsessional fiction that links science and pornography.
>
> *AE* 40

In *The Atrocity Exhibition* Ballard writes, "The geometry of the plaza exercised a unique fascination upon Talbot's mind" (*AE* 25). The obsession of Talbot with the location of the assassination and the geometry of the plaza, the landscape of this iconic moment, is an aspect of the novel that can also be seen as influenced by the *Warren Commission Report*, with its "chapters covering the exact relationships between the cardboard boxes on the seventh floor of the Book Depository" and "the bullet trajectories and speed of the Presidential limo" (*AE* 40). The specific geometry of Dealey Plaza and the trajectory of the shots are gone over in obsessive detail in the report, with several diagrams illustrating various angles and points of view. As Ballard stated regarding the Warren Report, "there's an obsessive concentration on the little details" (*R/SJGB* 10). This obsessive concentration on details in the report is transposed onto the figure of the T-character in *The Atrocity Exhibition* and his obsession with the events of the assassination, specifically with recreating small details through many re-enactments of the incident, "Trabert moved behind the steering wheel of the open limousine. Behind the empty jump seats the plastic mannequins of the President and his wife sat in the rear of the car [...] Holding in his hand the commercial replica of agent Greer's driving license he had bought in the arcade near the overpass [...]" (*AE* 74). The T-character re-enacts the assassination throughout the text, with slight variations in detail, such as the addition of Nurse Nagamatzu in the role of Jackie Kennedy, complete with a black wig (*AE* 49). The presence of the Japanese nurse in the re-enactment casts the assassination in the light of the greater malaise of the twentieth-century, in which the advent of nuclear fission plays a central role and further connects the text to "The Terminal Beach,"

> **Venus Smiles.** The dead face of the President's widow looked up at him from the track. Confused by the Japanese cast of her features, with all their reminders of Nagasaki and Hiroshima, he stared at the bowl of the telescope.
>
> *AE* 49

The merging of the assassination with the atomic bombs at Hiroshima and Nagasaki is a clear representation of Ballard's concern in *The Atrocity Exhibition* with the cultural landscape of the twentieth-century and also demonstrates the influence both of the *Warren Commission Report* and of *Operation Crossroads* on *The Atrocity Exhibition*, meshing as it does the key concerns of both these texts: the assassination and the atomic bomb. Ballard's text, in its many re-enactments and focus on different details, asserts the multiplicity of possible interpretations of historical events, and the connections that can be made.

The subtlest change in point of view alters the message of the official texts dramatically and demonstrates that small details can alter the manner in which significant cultural events are interpreted. It is the possibilities of just such a subtle alteration that Ballard explores in *The Atrocity Exhibition*. Subtle changes have the ability to recast narratives and this is demonstrated very clearly in the controversy over the reversal of significant frames from the Abraham Zapruder film which famously captured the assassination of John F. Kennedy, and was subsequently used a major piece of evidence during the Warren Commission investigation. As David Lubin discusses,

> More suspicious, in the view of critics, was the Report's reversal of the two frames that immediately follow number 313, which is the frame depicting the moment of the fatal head wound. Opponents of the commission's findings have argued that the order of these two frames is absolutely crucial to determining whether the president was initially thrown forward at the bullets' impact or thrown back against his seat, information they allege would indicate whether the bullet came from behind (that is, from Oswald in the School Book Depository) or from the front (from a second sniper positioned somewhere above the Grassy Knoll). (164)

This confusion over the running order of the frames of the Zapruder film is a perfect example of how the slightest change in detail can transform narratives and drastically alter the interpretation of a historic event. The obsession in *The Atrocity Exhibition* with re-enacting traumatic events from twentieth-century popular culture such as the assassination of Kennedy, in an effort to re-imagine them in a way which makes sense, is a clear commentary on this fluidity of meaning and interpretation, and a challenge to the authoritative and definitive narratives of official discourse such as the *Warren Commission Report*.

The *Warren Commission Report* demonstrates the desire to frame the iconic event of the assassination of Kennedy in an explicable and understandable narrative, expressing an authoritative desire to provide the truth,

> These conclusions represent the reasoned judgment of all members of the Commission and are presented after an investigation which has satisfied the Commission that it has ascertained the truth concerning the assassination of President Kennedy.
>
> *Warren Commission Report*

The authoritative and definitive presentation of facts in the text is something that is questioned throughout *The Atrocity Exhibition*, with Ballard's text refusing linear narratives and definitive interpretations of the assassination through its many different re-enactments. The disruption of linear narratives in *The Atrocity Exhibition* is a further embodiment of the "zone of non-time" of "The Terminal Beach," with the text becoming a zone out of time in which iconic events can be replayed and re-imagined, and new meanings and interpretations manifested.

The obsession of the central T-character with re-enacting the assassination is clearly linked to the *Warren Commission Report* in which a large section is devoted to a re-enactment of the presidential motorcade based on the footage of the Zapruder film,

> Substantial light has been shed on the assassination by viewing these motion pictures, particularly the Zapruder film [...] To pinpoint their locations, a man stood at Zapruder's position and directed the automobile and both models to the positions shown on each frame [...].
>
> *Warren Commission Report*

The re-enactment of the assassination in the *Warren Commission Report* is laid out frame by frame in the text and compared with frames from the Zapruder film. As David Culbert writes,

> The Warren Commission found the Zapruder footage so compelling that they used the film's 18.3 frames per second to re-enact the assassination. That is, they started with the shot that blows Kennedy's head apart, and worked backwards. (428)

This basing of a re-enactment on film footage is a double displacement of the event, pushing reality further into fiction, and Ballard displaces the narrative further in *The Atrocity Exhibition* through the various re-imaginings of the assassination. Indeed, Ballard described the *Warren Commission Report* as "[t]he novelization of the Zapruder film" (*UGM* 277), demonstrating further his interest in the reliance of the Commission on the "unimpeachable witness" (Lubin 171) of the film. Jeannette Baxter has commented on Ballard's questioning of the *Warren Commission Report*'s reliance on the visual record of the Zapruder footage,

> The Warren Report's meticulous autopsy of Zapruder's cine-film, which presumed the transparency of the medium and which read the visual image as an absolute, authentic and reliable source of documentation, is ordered in a strict chronological sequence; it is a narrative moving all too desperately towards neatness, coherency and closure which chooses to ignore (or exploit) the vulnerability of the medium which it rewrites. (95)

Ballard's text also seeks to exploit the vulnerability of visual mediums, demonstrating the fluidity of a visual image once it is manipulated, through the images on billboards in *The Atrocity Exhibition*, in which landscapes of the human body become abstract geometric forms,

> Looking at it more closely, Dr Nathan realized that in fact it was an immensely magnified portion of the skin over the iliac crest. Glancing at the billboards, Dr Nathan recognized other magnified fragments: a segment of lower lip, a right nostril, a portion of female perineum. Only an anatomist would have identified these fragments, each represented as a formal geometric pattern.
>
> *AE* 11

Ballard describes the re-enactments of tragic events in the text, such as the assassination of Kennedy, the death of Marilyn Monroe and the deaths of the three *Apollo* astronauts, as "Alternate Deaths" that "represent [the T-character's] attempt to make sense of these unhappy events and attribute to them a moral dimension and even, perhaps, a measure of hope" (AE 90). For Ballard, to make sense of these traumatic events is not to come to the cohesive historical narrative for which the *Warren Commission Report* strives, but rather to embody the myriad alternative readings of the event and to reveal the multiplicity of possible interpretations. Governmental publications such as the *Warren Commission Report*, strive to create a unifying narrative of iconic events such as the death of Kennedy, endeavouring to control the story in order to maintain the status quo. The *Warren Commission Report* wishes to draw a line under the tragedy and to enact a forgetting facilitated by an officially sanctioned explanation of the trauma. Ballard's texts implicitly question such desire for closure and cohesion, and indeed the ability to find a clear explanation for cultural trauma. *The Atrocity Exhibition* asserts that the iconic moment of the Kennedy assassination, as well as further iconic events of the twentieth-century such as the nuclear bomb, the Cold War and the Vietnam War, are symptoms of a greater societal malaise and landscape of cultural trauma that must be interrogated in order to be understood, and Ballard performs this interrogation through the repetition, re-enactment, juxtaposition and narrative fragmentation.

Ballard's texts interpret the assassination of Kennedy and the advent of nuclear weaponry as transformative moments in modern history, part of the "immense synthesis of the historical and psychic zero" (*CSS2* 32). These iconic moments and the landscapes in which they took place are zones of possibility for Ballard, representing as they do disruptions to the status quo, opportunities to step outside into zones of non-time. Ballard's texts emphasize the lure of the landscapes of iconic events and the significance these sites retain in cultural memory, preserving a residue of the events which took place there both in a physical sense, and, perhaps more significantly, in a psychological sense. In his notes to *The Atrocity Exhibition*, Ballard writes of the assassination:

> Special Agent William R. Greer of the Secret Service was the driver of the Presidential limousine. One can't help wondering how the events in Dealey Plaza affected him. Had his sense of space and time been altered?
> AE 40

For Ballard then, events of traumatic impact, such as the assassination of Kennedy, have the power to alter one's "sense of space and time," not just for those immediately involved in the incident, but for the modern psyche as a whole. Ballard asserts that "we were all in a sense in the driver's seat on that day in Dallas" (AE 40), given the very public nature of Kennedy's death and the subsequent media coverage of the event. In the aftermath of the shooting, "Television networks took over for four consecutive days of broadcasting on all three networks. All entertainment programming was cancelled. No commercial spots ran" (Barnhurst and Nerone 88) in a weekend that went on to feature the shooting of Lee Harvey Oswald live on television and the broadcast of Kennedy's funeral. The residue of iconic events thus remains not only in the physical landscapes of Dealey Plaza and the Pacific Island locations of the atomic bomb tests, but in the cultural landscape as events which transformed society's perception of humanity and its capabilities, and even of space and time, a rich opportunity which Ballard explores to the full in *The Atrocity Exhibition*.

In many ways, the landscape of *The Atrocity Exhibition* is reflective of the landscape of Ballard's library collection, meshing together various seemingly disparate elements such as Art (Surrealism in particular), Science, Architecture and History or Cultural Studies. The library itself can be compared to the free-association lists which make up much of the text of *The Atrocity Exhibition*, by putting very different items side-by-side and exploring the transformations which occur to meaning and interpretation through the juxtaposition. This essay has focused on just two of the many items of invisible literature in Ballard's library collection to explore the role of official historical narratives in the creation of "The Terminal Beach" and *The Atrocity Exhibition*. Ballard's use of texts such as *Operation Crossroads* and the *Warren Commission Report* is indicative of his diverse engagement with his library, at times using it as a source of thematic inspiration, re-appropriated found text, and as a stylistic template for his literary style. This invisible literature forms a visual, thematic and formal inspiration for the creation of Ballard's texts, and contributes to the experimental representation of the landscape of the twentieth century in *The Atrocity Exhibition*.

Works Cited

Barnhurst, Kevin G., and John C. Nerone. "The President is Dead: American News Photography and the New Long Journalism." In *Picturing the Past*. Edited by Bonnie Brennan and Hanno Hardt. Urbana: University of Illinois Press, 1999. 60–92.

Baxter, Jeannette. *J.G. Ballard's Surrealist Imagination: Spectacular Authorship*. Farnham: Ashgate, 2009.

Culbert, David. "Public Diplomacy and the International History of the Mass Media: The USIA, The Kennedy Assassination, and The World." *Historical Journal of Film, Radio and Television* 30 (2010): 421–432.

Derrida, Jacques. *Archive Fever: A Freudian Impression*. Chicago and London: The University of Chicago Press, 1996.

Fraser, Antonia. *The Pleasure of Reading*. London: Bloomsbury, 1992.

Freshwater, Helen. "The Allure of the Archive." *Poetics Today* 24:4 (2003): 729–758. *Project Muse*. Web. 29 September 2011.

Gasiorek, Andrzej. *J.G. Ballard*. Manchester: Manchester University Press, 2005.

Joint Task Force One, The Office of the Historian. *Operation Crossroads: The Official Pictorial Record*. New York: Wm. H. Wise and Co Inc, 1946.

Lubin, David. *Shooting Kennedy: JFK and the Culture of Images*. Berkeley, Los Angeles and London: University of California Press, 2003.

Luckhurst, Roger. *"The Angle between Two Walls": The Fiction of J.G. Ballard*. Liverpool: Liverpool University Press, 1997.

Punter, David. *Literature of Terror: a history of Gothic fictions from 1765 to the present day. Vol. II*. London: Longman, 1996.

United States. Congress. House. Select Committee on Assassinations. *Final Report of the Select Committee on Assassinations, U.S. House of Representatives, Summary of Findings and Recommendations,* 95th Cong., 2nd sess. Report 95–1828. Washington: U.S. G.P.O. 1979. *National Archives*. The U.S. National Archives and Records Administration. Web. 9 June 2014.

United States. Assassinations Records Review Board. *Final Report of the Assassinations Records Review Board*, September 30th 1998, *JFK Assassination Records*, Washington: U.S. Govt. Print. Off., 1998, *National Archives*. The U.S. National Archives and Records Administration. Web. 9 June 2014.

United States. President's Commission on the Assassination of President John F. Kennedy. *The Official Warren Commission Report of the Assassination of the President John F. Kennedy*. Garden City, New York: Doubleday, 1964.

Zelizer, Barbie. *Covering the Body: The Kennedy Assassination, the Media, and the Shaping of Collective Memory*. Chicago: University of Chicago Press, 1992.

CHAPTER 4

Speeding to the Doldrums: Stalled Futures and the Disappearance of Tomorrow in "The Dead Astronaut"

Andrew Warstat

Abstract

This chapter discusses how J.G. Ballard's short story "The Dead Astronaut" is fixated on a melancholic and alienated future that never arrived. The narrative is, literally, a disaster story, containing astral traces of a dead or absent future. In Ballard's tale, the protagonist's return to this stalled future is premised on the absence or impossibility of a primal scene to return to: the future is inaccessible and has yet to happen. Instead of productively mourning one particular version of the future (which might then provoke further futures), the story melancholically reiterates a stalled, traumatic process of *nachträglichkeit* or "coming after." What, the chapter asks, does Ballard's story tell us about our impulsion or compulsion towards the future? Is the text the narrative of an interminable post-modern stasis, of "dialectics at a standstill"? Or does it allegorise what happens in the commodification of the future?

Keywords

J.G. Ballard – short fiction – science fiction – future – melancholy – repetition – trauma – alienation – *nachträglichkeit* – critical theory – Marxism – Freud

> Does the future still have a future?
>
> BALLARD, *UGM* 192

Projecting unrealized versions of what may happen next, whether positive or negative, defines science fiction. The genre is preoccupied with imagining possible worlds or alternative futures. However, the narrative content of science fiction will never, regardless of its complexity or ambition, simply take the form of a forecast.

Speculative fiction does not appear as news from nowhere. The production of ideas and stories about possible futures always arises from historically specific contexts. Any image of the future will appear within a dynamic aesthetic, social, political and historical environment that both allows and restricts imaginative possibilities. This is the case even when the imagination is being pushed to the limits of what can (currently) be imagined.

Examining the limits of speculative creativity raises questions about causality. What makes us imagine the future this way rather than that? What stops us imagining something different?[1] As a consequence, alternative conceptions of the future always implicitly indicate what the present is, and is not, imaginatively capable of. As Franco Berardi notes in his book *After the Future*: "The future is not a natural dimension of the mind. It is a modality of projection and imagination, a feature of expectation and attention, and its modalities and features change with the changing of cultures" (28).

J.G. Ballard's writing was preoccupied with the future: the future as a psychological dystopia, as a place already decaying, as a place stalled and inaccessible.[2] Such themes are obviously apparent in a text like *The Atrocity Exhibition* (1970) with Ballard noting how in late capitalist modernity we are "[d]esperate for the new, but disappointed with anything but the familiar", leading us to constantly "recolonize past and future" (*AE* 88). Reading "The Dead Astronaut", published two years earlier than *The Atrocity Exhibition*, it is possible to see how and why Ballard's exploration of the future leads not to a programmatic forecast, but to an ambivalent re-calibration of what the process of futurological speculation, *in itself*, actually means in an historical era where there seems to be no future, or where the future is simply more of the same.[3]

Ballard's short story can be read for multiple symptoms of the nature of time in modernity. Here, though, we can consider two key signs or tropes about time and the future. Firstly, it's possible to examine how the story is structurally premised on trauma and that this trauma is something that happens in the

---

1   See, for example, Fredric Jameson's discussion of temporal and historical development in his essay "The Barrier of Time" in *Archaeologies of the Future* (85–106).

2   For a fascinating examination of how Ballard's exploration of time can be read in relation to psychological disturbance in the stories "News from the Sun" (*CSS2* 531–568), "Memories of the Space Age" (*CSS2* 569–601) and "Myths of the Near Future" (*CSS2* 602–634), see Mike Holliday's "Ballard and the Vicissitudes of Time".

3   For an intriguing, radically different reading of "The Dead Astronaut" (offering an ultimately more optimistic, post-humanist/Deleuzian account of the conclusion of the narrative, informed in part by Donna Harraway's work on science fiction) see Melanie Rosen Brown's "Dead Astronauts, Cyborgs, and the Cape Canaveral Fiction of J.G. Ballard: A Posthuman Analysis". Also of importance in the secondary literature on Ballard's "Cape Canaveral" fictions is Umberto Rossi's "A Little Something About Dead Astronauts", which deals with a number of Ballard's short stories that figure the death of astronauts.

background history of the narrative that forever alters how things happen in the future. Secondly, as a result of this event or non-event, both historical development and narrative development in the text becomes trapped or circular. Modernity as a better future, a place of coherent resolution, stability, definitive closure and meaning, the dream of a certain liberal, bourgeois society, doesn't happen. Instead past events keep repeating in the present. In psychoanalytic terms, we could say that the story is like a patient undergoing therapy, who is encouraged to work through what happened to them in order to move on, but is unable to achieve that outcome. Essentially the patient and the story are stuck.

As a result, Ballard's fiction can be read as an account of what we will call late capitalist modernity's melancholic (as opposed to mourned) and ensnared relationship to the future. The wider, critical significance of this melancholia is that it indicates an exhaustion with a certain type of speculative imagination, an exhaustion within modernity that, at one level, haunts any prospective vision of the future. This is something that Mark Fisher describes when he writes that "the slow cancellation of the future has been accompanied by a deflation of expectations" (25). Ballard's fictions meditate and focus on cultural, social, chronological and psychological forms of collapse and fatigue. His work, therefore, acts as an exemplary challenge to Berardi's claim that "exhaustion plays no role in the imagination of modernity" (44).

1968 and All That

The historical context for Ballard's story is significant. "The Dead Astronaut" was first published in May 1968. The text itself first appeared in the May edition of *Playboy* (Ballard, *Playboy* 118). The previous year, the oil embargo hinted at the coming energy crisis and shifts in how industrialized, western economies operated were also apparent. There was, for example, a decline in employment in manufacturing industries in the United Kingdom, presaging the dialectic of de-industrialization, globalization and the growth of service sector employment. More specifically pertinent to the story, Apollo 1, which was planned as the first manned flight of the Apollo programme, caught fire on the launch-pad killing all three of the crew.

The story appears, then, in a wider historical context of change, where the possibility for another type of future was palpable and real.[4] One of the most

---

4 It is worth noting the connection Fredric Jameson makes between Ballard's lost protagonists, devastated landscapes and stories of disrupted history. Jameson has suggested that the main

striking historical disjunctions of Ballard's story is that, whilst it was written a year before the actual Apollo 11 moon landing, the story imagines the future as already played out and exhausted. The historical nature of that future, what actually happened next, was, therefore, actually much more ambivalent. Retrospectively, we might say that the kind of historical change actually occurring was the development of our world, a place of neo-liberal capitalism, of disaffected individualism, technological alienation and globalized consumerism. This world is the place that Ballard's subsequent writing invariably focuses on.

"The Dead Astronaut" itself describes how the two protagonists, ex-NASA employees Judith and Phillip (with Phillip the narrator of the story), await the return to earth of a dead astronaut, Robert Hamilton, who was killed soon after launching into space 20 years before the incidents in the story. The protagonists were there at the launch and the death of Hamilton and they are there at the return of the spacecraft with the dead body, providing the narrative structure for the story.[5] The story also maps onto a more intimate aspect of the characters' story. Judith became obsessed by Hamilton, prior to his departure, and his death coincided with Judith's miscarriage. The story closes with the revelation that Hamilton was, in fact, the father of the child. The figure of Hamilton is, therefore, critical both to opening up and to closing down futures. These incidents demarcate and define Judith's character and explain why she becomes frozen in time, such that she would "stare at the bedroom clock, as if waiting for something to happen" (CSS2 263).

The story merges the collapse of the character's psychological state with the landscape in that the decaying mental status of the characters is reflected in the physical landscape of the deserted wasteland. The Florida launch site that Judith and Phillip return to has become the graveyard for the damaged satellites and rockets that have fallen back to earth. Phillip and Judith go to

---

historical, ideological key for reading these images and narratives in Ballard is the break-up of colonial empires and the development of post colonialism. See, for example, Jameson's comments in his essay "Journey Into Fear": "[It] does not seem out of place to interpret the immense eschatological *jouissance* of the greatest of modern apocalyptic writers, J.G. Ballard, as the expression of his experience of the end of the British Empire in the Second World War" (199).

5   The orbiting spacecraft of the dead astronaut(s) function, in a way, as traditional astrological symbols or stars in that they fulfill the role of predicting the future ("[...] their capsules [...] revolve through the night sky like the stars of a new constellation [...] the figure of this dead astronaut circling the sky above us re-emerged in her mind as an obsession with time" (CSS2 262–263). With the return to earth of the dead astronaut and the disappearance of the star, time and the future stop thereby heralding, literally, a disaster. This very specific sense of the word disaster draws out the etymology of the term and its link to the Latin roots concerning the negation of a star, *astrum*, and the sense that the sight of a failing comet was a bad omen.

the deserted wasteland when they hear that Hamilton is about to return to earth, in order to lay to rest the ghostly presence the astronaut has assumed in their lives. The conclusion of the story comes when, having reached Hamilton's crashed unit and recovered the remains, the protagonists start to suffer from radiation sickness, revealing that the spacecraft was in fact carrying atomic weapons, with the dead astronaut infecting the protagonists with his own version of technological death.

The narrative pattern that emerges is one of repetition, circularity and decay. Judith and Phillip's personal experience of loss of the unborn child is linked to the wider loss of the technologically advanced future and the failure of the space program. In both cases, the advent of a new period in time or history is marked by death or failure, with the narrative literally suspended between two deaths. And in terms of Ballard's story, what looks like the start of something new turns out to be a repetition and an inability to move on. The stilling or halting of the progression of time generates repetition and trauma for the protagonists.

Again, Do It Again

Repetition is not, of course, inherently sterile or negative. In one sense, repetition does indeed do good. In psychoanalysis, revisiting the past is essential for the person undergoing treatment as they learn to cope with living in the present. Freud, in his account of treating the wolf man, Sergei Pankeyev, invents a concept and narrative form to create meaning out of traumatic symptoms that occurred in the past. Freud's theoretical form seems to provide an explanation for how something witnessed in the past reappears and repeats in the present. This concept seems to explain how the unconscious may preserve a specific experience, while its traumatic after-effects might only be realized by another later, but associated, event. Freud called this *"nachträglichkeit"* which is variously translated into English as "deferred action" or "retrospective determination" (45–46).

This theory of deferred action, developed out of Freud's account of his analyses of the problem of sexuality in human development, reveals that a small child might well not immediately understand the significance of a sexual encounter or witnessed event. They would instead only come to understand this experience when they themselves became sexually active in adulthood.[6] The

---

6 For further analysis and development of the concept of *nachträglichkeit* see the work of Jean Laplanche and, specifically in relation to temporality and trauma, Cathy Caruth's interview with Laplanche in the journal *Postmodern Culture*.

reappearance or repetition of this past event would invariably occur, however, in a disconcerting or cryptic form, and failure to work through the source of the trauma would lead to being trapped in the past.

This process of "deferred action" can usefully serve as a way of describing the actions of the protagonists, but also the wider account of time that Ballard introduces. The repeated forms of death, the return to the "non place" of the ruined launch site, the fixation with and fear of technology can all be read as traumatic symptoms which, because they are only partially understood and comprehended at the time by the protagonists, lead to the suspension of time and meaning. The story therefore serves as a direct counter to Alfonso Cuarón's film *Gravity*, in which an astronaut's encounter with death (in this case stemming from the main character's distress after the death of her child) ultimately leads to a healing process and re-birth. The closing scene shows Cuarón's astronaut reborn, hopeful and rejuvenated, emerging from the sea.

In contrast, "The Dead Astronaut" is a story based around a frustrated process of *nachträglichkeit*. The story sets up the need for a retrospective deciphering across a delay in time. This is both in the sense that, coming to the end of the story one needs to re-read the text to overlay and triangulate interpretations because the implications of the account aren't immediately apparent, but also because the story's narrative is itself about delay.

In opposition to a conventional Freudian narrative resulting in a successful process of analysis, where the trauma is revisited and exorcized, Ballard's story erases its own primal scene. That is to say, as an attempt to revisit the grave of the future – the place where the space age died, the place where the characters' lives came to an end, the original starting point for the things that subsequently went wrong – the story is actually performative. The story is about an event that, in happening, alters how events themselves happen. That event isn't simply a chronological irregularity that can be examined via a therapeutic and linear process of retrospection. The character of the trauma alters the ability to move backwards and forwards in memory and time.

Ballard, addressing how time was disturbed by the trauma of the conjunction of death and space travel, asked in the *Atrocity Exhibition*:[7] "Why must we await, and fear, a disaster in space in order to understand our own time?" (*AE* 68). He answered:

---

7   Ballard here paraphrases and quotes the Chilean painter Roberto Matta in the catalogue
    notes for Matta's exhibition *Matta: Dis-Astronaute*.

> All disasters – earthquakes, plane or car crashes – seem to reveal for a brief moment the secret formulae of the world around us, but a disaster in space rewrites the rules of the continuum itself.
>
> *AE* 76

The disturbance introduced by the failure of the space age, manifested in this story by the death of the astronaut, breaks any trajectory of progress. Time, instead of going forward and advancing, becomes fractured and turns back on itself. An inability to access space literally affects time. In another of the so-called "Cape Canaveral" stories, *Myths of the Near Future*, the point is clearly made:

> This space sickness – it's really about time, not space, like all the Apollo flights. We think of it as a kind of madness, but in fact it may be a contingency plan laid down millions of years ago, a real space programme, a chance to escape into a world beyond time.
>
> *CSS2* 625

In "The Dead Astronaut", the reader is led to imagine a narrative pattern based on a structure similar to the eternal return. However, the return point (the point of origin, access to the living/dead astronaut Hamilton) is never actually reached because, of course, it never happened. The story is a work of imaginative fiction and the future on which the text is predicated never existed. So, whilst there may have been retrospective factual justification for Ballard's story, for example, in relation to atomic weapons,[8] the aporia that the story creates occurs primarily, or in the first instance, in the reader's imagination. The external trauma becomes transferred, relocated in the imagination and subconscious. As a result, any process of Freudian retrospective determination as an interpretive or therapeutic tool is, in Ballard's story, incomplete and uncompletable because time stops flowing in any comprehensible way.

Conflating this issue in the story with the historical context of the text, Ballard suggested, in an interview from the early 1980s, that "in many ways, time didn't exist in the sixties" but had become "a set of endlessly proliferating

---

8 In 1958 NASA planned, in *Project 119 – A Study of Lunar Research Flights,* to detonate an atomic bomb on the moon (Reiffel, "The Defense Technical Information Center"). The project remained secret until the mid-1990s when Keay Davidson, who was researching a biography of Carl Sagan, came across references to the project and found that Sagan had been involved in the research for Project 119.

presents" (Ballard, "The Art of Fiction" 133–160). Ballard went on to qualify this by saying that "time returned in the seventies, but not a sense of the future. The hands of the clock now [went] nowhere" (Ballard, "The Art of Fiction" 155). Ballard's general comment about the future might therefore recall the well-known British punk rock slogan of the 1970s from the Sex Pistols: "no future."

This is not to say that, today, novelty ceases to exist. We might consider for example the endless, but immediately stale, stream of new mobile phones. Rather, as Ross Wolfe has noted, the "ceaseless proliferation of the new now presents itself as the eternal return of the same old, same old. Novelty today has become quotidian, if not wholly antique [...] History of late may be going nowhere, but it's going nowhere faster" (Wolfe, "The Charnel-House: From Bauhaus to Beinhaus"). This process of nihilistic acceleration, involving more of the same, only faster and more intensely, has taken many different forms as recent accounts of singularity and the debates around accelerationism can confirm.[9] In Ballard's fiction, imagining the future via the disappearance of a space age that never really happened, is an engagement with a darker, deathly history with no future that is, paradoxically, the melancholic present. This is precisely the problem: that both Ballard's "now" and future are melancholic.

The Melancholia of Now

"The Dead Astronaut" takes melancholia as its subject and style. Referring to Freud again and his distinction between mourning and melancholia, one can

---

9   In a limited sense, technological singularity describes a prediction whereby the processing and computing power of artificial intelligence will exceed human intelligence and herald a post-human era via the fusion of the biological and technological. Accounts and predictions of this event can be found in the work of mathematicians, technologists and futurologists such as Ray Kurzweil and Vernor Vinge ("The Coming Technological Singularity"). Specific predictions about dates for this event (Kurzweil has proposed that singularity will occur in the next 25 years) have, however, been described by writers such as Steven Shaviro as being based on "dubious premises". Shaviro's comments about singularity ("The Singularity is Here" Bould & Miéville 103–117) and the ever-increasing role of technology in accounts of the future come, however, within the context of debates about Deleuzian post-humanism and accelerationism. Accelerationism has been developed from certain texts in Lyotard, Deleuze and Guattari and other thinkers with the suggestion that, in order to set in motion the conditions for a revolutionary change in society, heralding a profound revision of what the future could be, "capital should not be resisted but accelerated" (see Centre for Cultural Studies for an overview of the 2010 conference on accelerationism and Wolf for a recording of the proceedings). Ballard's writing has been deployed and used in the work of thinkers both associated with and critical of accelerationism (Brassier "The Catastrophe of Time" and MoMA PS1).

say that, if Ballard's story worked through the process of loss in accordance with the process of mourning, the result would have been a narrative about the successful resolution of the traumatic events it deals with closer to that of Cuarón's film. This is because, for Freud, mourning describes the difficult but fundamentally healthy way in which a person copes with loss via tradition, custom, culture and psychic wellbeing. Melancholia, in contrast, occurs when there is confusion about what, exactly, has been lost. According to Freud, in melancholia "the [missing] object has not perhaps actually died, but has been lost as an object of love" (244) a description which fits, almost too perfectly, both the inter-personal relations of the characters in Ballard's story, and also a wider social engagement with technology. Freud continued his definition, however, by claiming that, in melancholia, "one feels justified in maintaining the belief that a loss [...] has occurred, but one cannot see clearly what it is that has been lost" such that "melancholia is in some way related to an object-loss which is withdrawn from consciousness, in contradistinction to mourning, in which there is nothing about the loss that is unconscious" (244).

An inability to "think through" the trauma of absence results in the transference of loss into the unconscious, freezing progress. The result, in the story, is that the protagonists become stuck in time. Ballard's characters are like Durer's depressed, lethargic angel *Melancholia* (1514) or Walter Benjamin's melancholic seraphim,[10] only now these heavenly angels need to be taken as symbols for the figure of the astronaut. Like Benjamin and Klee's angel, Ballard's protagonists suffer the effects of being caught in the winds of progress, trapped by death and destruction.

The unresolvable cause of the melancholia of the story is the distress caused by an absent future that never materializes. For Berardi, writing from a Marxist perspective, the wider social and political source of this melancholia is the "rise of the myth of the future [which] is rooted in modern capitalism, in the experience of expansion of the economy and knowledge. The idea that the future will be better than the present is not a natural idea, but the imaginary effect of the peculiarity of the bourgeois production model" (22).

The future offered by this socio-economic imaginary, with which Ballard's work is invariably fixated, has consistently failed to materialize and is, in fact, structurally unable to materialize since the defining motor of capitalism is an

---

10   Walter Benjamin, writing in *Theses on the Philosophy of History*, found the spirit of progress visualized in Paul Klee's 1920 painting *Angelus Novus* (245–255).

insatiable desire to generate abstract value, profit and never-ending growth. It is the perennially absent future of capitalism, currently appearing as neo-liberalism, that is our present: a time which has been drained of any cultural imagination capable of reinventing the utopian as a viable alternative to an interminable now. As Theodor Adorno noted: "The future bows before the omnipotence of the present" (117).

This absent future was a tangible issue for Ballard: "There's something missing from the world that we all inhabit [...] We've lost our faith in the far future, and [...] we're living in a commodified world where everything has a price-tag. A world filled with dreams that money can buy, but dreams that soon pall" (Ballard & Self, 2006). The promise of a future defined by space travel offered no respite: "Looking back, we can see that far from extending forever into the future, the space age lasted for scarcely fifteen years: from Sputnik and Gagarin's first flight in 1961 to the last Skylab mission in 1974" (UGM 224–225). As a consequence of the absence of any historical or cultural dynamic to offer anything different, boredom and psychopathology became necessary and fascinating: "[...] Being quite serious, the future may be boring. It's possible that my children and yours will live in an eventless world, and that the faculty of imagination will die, or express itself solely in the realm of psychopathology" (Ballard, "The Art of Fiction" 155).

The result is that the utopian future exists as a negative possibility: we are aware of it because of its absence. The paradox is that this absence is imprinted into the social and technological imagination of capitalist modernity. This negation of the utopian impulse and its relocation in the social unconscious is the missing primal scene or drive at work in Ballard's story:

> Did the future arrive too soon, some time around the mid-century, the greatest era of modern science fiction? It has always struck me as remarkable that one of the twentieth century's greatest achievements, Neil Armstrong's landing on the Moon, a triumph of courage and technology, should have had virtually no influence on the world at large.
>
> UGM 192

The absent future has no positive influence on the "world at large"; instead it demarcates an unthinkable zone in our technological, socio-political imaginary. Fredric Jameson, commenting more generally about science fiction, noted that "what is indeed authentic about it, as a mode of narrative and a form of knowledge, is not [...] its capacity to keep the future alive, even in imagination. On the contrary, its deepest vocation is over and over again to demonstrate and to dramatize our incapacity to imagine the future" (288).

Works Cited

Adorno, Theodor. *Prisms*. Translated by Samuel Weber and Shierry Weber. Cambridge, MA: MIT Press, 1997.

Ballard, J.G. "The Dead Astronaut". *Playboy* (May 1968): 160.

Ballard, J.G. and Thomas Frick. "Interviews: The Art of Fiction". *Paris Review* 94 (1984): 133–160.

Benjamin, Walter. *Illuminations*. Edited by Hannah Arendt. Translated by Harry Zohn. London: Vintage, 1999.

Berardi, Franco 'Bifo.' *After the Future*. Translated by Arianna Bove, et al. Edinburgh: AK Press, 2011.

Bould, Mark and China Miéville. *Red Planets: Marxism and Science Fiction*. Middletown: Pluto Press and Wesleyan University Press, 2009.

Brassier, Ray. "The Catastrophe of Time". Presentation at Staatliche Hochschule für Bildende Künste, 2013.

Brassier, Ray. MoMA PS1 Events. 19 July 2013. Web. 26 August 2014.

Brown, Melanie Rosen. "Dead Astronauts, Cyborgs, and the Cape Canaveral Fiction of J.G. Ballard: A Posthuman Analysis". *Reconstruction: Studies in Contemporary Culture* 4:3 (2004). Web. 26 August 2014.

Caruth, Cathy and Jean Laplanche. "An Interview with Jean Laplanche". *Postmodern Culture* 11:2 (2001). Web. 26 August 2014.

CCS, Goldsmiths. Goldsmiths, University of London, Centre for Cultural Studies. 26 May 2010. Web. 26 August 2014.

Cuarón, Alfonso. (Dir.) *Gravity*. Warner Brothers Pictures (2013).

Davidson, Keay. *Carl Sagan: A Life*. New York: John Wiley, 1999.

Echaurren, Roberto Sebastian Antonio Matta. *Matta: Dis-Astronaute*. New York: Alexander Iolas Gallery, 1966.

Fisher, Mark. *Ghosts of My Life: Writings on Depression, Hauntology and Lost Futures*. Winchester: Zero Books, 2014.

Freud, Sigmund. *The Standard Edition of the Complete Psychological Works of Sigmund Freud*. Edited by James Strachey and Anna Freud et al. Translated by James Strachey. London and Toronto: The Hogarth Press, 1955.

Freud, Sigmund. *The Standard Edition of the Complete Psychological Works of Sigmund Freud, Volume XIV (1914–1916): On the History of the Psycho-Analytic Movement, Papers on Metapsychology and Other Works*. Edited by James Strachey. London: Hogarth, 1957.

Holliday, Mike. "Ballard and the Vicissitudes of Time". *Ballardian*, 3 July 2008 Web. 24 August 2014.

Jameson, Fredric. *Archaeologies of the Future: The Desire Called Utopia and Other Science Fictions*. London: Verso, 2005.

Reiffel, L. "The Defense Technical Information Center". Defense Technical Information Center. Illinois Institute for Technology; NASA, 19 June 1959. Web. 19 August 2014.

Rossi, Umberto. "A Little Something about Dead Astronauts". *Science Fiction Studies* 36:107 (2009). Web. 24 August 2014.

Self, Will. "Archive on 4: Self On Ballard". BBC Radio 4, 2006. Web. 20 August 2014.

Shaviro, Steven. "Accelerando." 13 October 2005. Web. 26 August 2014.

Vinge, Vernor. "The Coming Technological Singularity: How to Survive in the Post-Human Era". ROHAN Academic Computing – Vernor Vinge home page. 30 March 1993. San Diego State University. Web. 26 August 2014.

Williams, Alex and Nick Srnicek. "Critical Legal Thinking – Law & the Political". 14 May 2013. Web. 26 August 2014.

Wolf, René. "Backdoor Broadcasting – Accelerationism". Web. 26 August 2014.

Wolfe, Ross. "The Charnel-House: From Bauhaus to Beinhaus". 10 August 2012. Web. 23 August 2014.

CHAPTER 5

Jarry, Joyce and the Apocalyptic Intertextuality of *The Atrocity Exhibition*

Richard Brown

Abstract

This chapter investigates *The Atrocity Exhibition*, a novel that shows Ballard's writing in its most experimental form. The chapter analyses the tendency of the text to work through a literary landscape of intertextuality, moving away from conventional narrative mimesis. Such apocalyptic intertextuality involves the reader in encounters with a directly acknowledged precursor such as Surrealist Alfred Jarry, with the extreme assortments of material in the collections of "Terminal Documents" that occur through the text and in a reassessment of his complex relationship with one-time "wordmaster" James Joyce.

Keywords

J.G. Ballard – *The Atrocity Exhibition* – Apocalyptic intertextuality – literary relations – Alfred Jarry – James Joyce – the *avant-garde*

The landscape of *The Atrocity Exhibition* is as much an intertextual as it is a physical landscape and it is characterized by an apocalyptic intertextuality whose experimental range takes in literary and popular cultures, visual art works, cinema, advertising, architecture, media and magazine journalism, government reports and science. Surrealism in the mode of mad science is regularly acknowledged in criticism, in Ballard's work itself and in Ballard's notes, as the book's way of trying to make sense of the madness of the contemporary world. The transforming, modular subjectivity of its "bizarre jigsaw" (*AE* 130) protagonist, variously named Travis, Talbot and so on, the T-figure, and his "disquieting" experiments, personal relationships and their surveillance by Dr Nathan and Catherine Austin, make up the more traditional narrative core of the text.[1] Yet that narrative thread becomes more complex and opaque,

---

1 Luckhurst (73–117) and Baxter (59–98) provide two of the strongest critical readings of the text whilst inevitably leaving much of its material still to be explored.

and as it does the reader is increasingly likely to attempt to understand its world through its intertextual frames. By exploring one thread of this intertextuality we can revisit aspects of Ballard's relationship with an acknowledged early twentieth-century *avant-garde* precursor. Alongside such acknowledged points of reference in the text itself, I argue here, we can discern a complex and ambiguous relationship with Ballard's one-time "wordmaster" James Joyce,[2] who, though not explicitly acknowledged as a direct source in the text or notes, sits behind its experimental trajectories in significant ways.

The final section of *The Atrocity Exhibition* illustrates an example of its intertextuality, explicitly reworking a source text from Ballard's favourite territory of the early twentieth-century *avant-garde*, one that is itself quite pointedly apocalyptic in its Surrealist inversion of Biblical text. This is "The Assassination of John Fitzgerald Kennedy Considered as a Downhill Motor Race" (*AE* 171–3) which is a direct recasting of the outrageous Surrealist prose work by Alfred Jarry, "The Crucifixion Considered as an Uphill Bicycle Race." In the context of *The Atrocity Exhibition* as a whole, Ballard's final chapter may be understood as one of many bizarre attempts to understand the absurdity of the Kennedy assassination, to "kill Kennedy again but in a way that makes sense" (*AE* 50), in this case in an absurd juxtaposition with the absurdity of accelerated motor-car culture and that of the media circus of the presidential "race." In something like traditional plot terms, it seems to originate more specifically from the mysterious student Koester in the "University of Death" section who plots scenarios of Talbot's death. He refers to what he calls "Jarry's piece of happy anti-clericalism" (*AE* 29) in conversation with Catherine Austin and Dr Nathan observes Koester's "optimized auto-fatality, conceived by the driver as some kind of bizarre crucifixion" gesturing towards the title of a Dali picture in describing it as "Christ crucified on the sodomized body of his own mother" (*AE* 31). Yet by the final chapters, the attempts of most readers to hold on to the detailed threads of a conventional T-figure plot will have been challenged or effectively replaced by a sense of the obtrusive and unsettling impact of the intertextual exercise itself as the short story fragments are set adrift from the semblances of conventional narrative material that remain only in synoptic headlines in the final sections.

Those readers who accept the invitation to explore Jarry's original, will find a fine example of his *avant-garde* pseudo-science of "pataphysics" which explicitly proposed to account for the irrationality of the world through deliberately irrational ideas. Ballard quite probably knew it from its publication in English in Roger Shattuck and Simon Taylor's *Selected Works of Alfred Jarry*,

---

2   This is the phrase used by Ballard in the self-authored December 1956 *New Worlds* profile of his work discussed below.

which came out in 1965 as Ballard's literary career trajectory was becoming established. The wording of the title in that translation is not the "crucifixion" of Ballard's later explanatory author's note but "passion" (122–4) as it is in his review of the books on Surrealism by Patrick Waldberg and Marcel Jean published in *New Worlds* in 1966 (*UGM* 85). In Jarry's absurd version of the "passion," St. Matthew is a sports journalist, Christ is a racing cyclist who suffers a puncture from his crown of thorns so has to carry his cross-framed bike on his shoulder up the hill-climb race to Golgotha. Pilate is the time-keeper, Barabbas is another competitor who is scratched from the race, the two thieves take the lead, there are various crashes, there is no apparent winner and Christ eventually continues the race airborne. Jarry's text is apocalyptic in that it juxtaposes the sacred New Testament narrative with the secular modern discourse of sports journalism, inviting unsettling questions about that distinction as about the continuity or otherwise of such narrative paradigms and the modes of consciousness and civilization supposedly common to both.

Ballard's final section is a surprisingly close reworking of this original (however marked by incongruity they both are) with the uphill bicycle race turned into a downhill car race and Kennedy and Johnson as Presidential and Vice-Presidential contenders. Lee Harvey Oswald is the starter who "misfires" and is given the blame by a Warren Commission Report which appears here as a cynically commercial "rake-off on the book of the race" (*AE* 173). The Jarry template is offered as an absurd alternative to the model of apparent rationality which the American government's official report attempted to provide. Ballard's provocative author's note presents the Report itself as "a work of fiction" (*AE* 40) apparently offering his reworked version of Jarry as an absurd alternative in order to expose this. Deliberate confusions of fact and fiction have also underpinned the various creative and/or scientific "studies" undertaken by the patients and/or scientists of the "Institute" who make up Ballard's novel's strange world.

However complex the use of Jarry in this section might appear, it is, in one sense, quite straightforward, inasmuch as Ballard's intertextuality here depends on a sustained relationship with a single original text. Yet more characteristic of the intertextual landscape of *The Atrocity Exhibition* as a whole may be its refusal to privilege links with any single text or even kinds of text, and to offer instead a deliberately unsettling array of cultural and textual references which at once deploy and unsettle the category of the literary. In this respect its intertextuality looks beyond the Jarry model.

One reference point for the sheer mixedness of this intertextual landscape might be found at the start of the text itself in the form of Travis's assembly of seven numbered "terminal documents," including astronomical, architectural and geological images, Marey's Chronograms, the desert landscape of the Qattara Depression, Max Ernst's Surrealist "Garden Airplane Traps" and "fusing sequences" for the Hiroshima and Nagasaki atomic bombs (*AE* 1–2). Travis's "terminal documents" are partly scientific, partly cultural, partly historical, and together form a deliberately random or experimental assemblage of evidence for something they may or may not be able to account for or explain. In that respect they resemble the art work of the patients in the exhibition that gives the section and the novel its title, and may be as much symptoms as they are representations of the "atrocity" they depict. They seem to form an impossibly dysmorphic jigsaw puzzle of cultural reference points, which define the T-figure's traumatized postmodern subjectivity and the various activities of Dr Nathan's Institute in trying to piece together some kind of meaning in a traumatically meaningless world.

In the subsection of the "The Atrocity Exhibition" section that is itself named "The Atrocity Exhibition" we find another assembly of images which includes the atrocities of Vietnam and the Congo "mimetised" in the imagined death of screen actress Elizabeth Taylor, the verandas of the London Hilton (a new building in 1963 and still controversial) and, once again, Max Ernst, here culminating in the literary image of the human race as "Caliban asleep across a mirror smeared with vomit" (*AE* 12). Paradoxically this reference to a Shakespearean character, might highlight the extent to which the literary, at least in its conventional sense, remains present even though it may no longer dominate the intertextual landscape. In this section the protagonist (here unnamed and uncannily resembling the bomber pilot who may be the surviving traumatized Nagasaki A-bomb pilot Claude Eatherly) emerges to sing with a "beat group" named "The Him" whose rhythms echo the "beat" of the Sikorski helicopter overhead (*AE* 136, 132) suggesting a media landscape which is defined by scientific and technological innovation and popular music. Throughout the text it is a cultural landscape that is less a cohesive "monoculture" (*UGM* 89), whether literary or popular, and more characterized by that memorable phrase in the title of the fourteenth subsection of the first chapter as "The Lost Symmetry of the Blastosphere" (*AE* 8).

Undoubtedly extreme, the cultural landscape of Ballard's text at times resembles the menacing intentions of the students of the institute whose "terminal documents" are said at one point to "constitute an assassination weapon" (*AE* 47) albeit, as the next subsection goes on to extrapolate, "[n]ot in the sense you mean" (*AE* 47). Its world frequently recalls that of the 1919 expressionist film *The Cabinet of Dr Caligari* (mentioned by Ballard in a review, *UGM* 90), in which madness is embraced and, in the film's famous twist ending, the borders between the supposedly mad patient and the supposedly sane doctor deliberately transgressed.

In the authorial note to "You and Me and the Continuum," Ballard himself comments that: "Readers will have noticed that, in contrast, there are almost no references to literary works" (AE 139). Yet this is clearly an exaggeration. Though always keen to unsettle literary pieties, Ballard's fiction and critical writings and what we know of his personal library from published sources,[3] inevitably engage the literary work, whether in a dependence on canonical literary writers from Daniel Defoe to Joseph Conrad, in his knowledgeable references to lesser-known *avant-garde* and Surrealist writers from Raymond Roussel (AE 91, 99) to Ann Quin (AE 145) and indeed to such received modernist literary writers as Joyce, Eliot and Woolf, even if he sometimes sees them as "introverted" in contrast to Kafka or H.G. Wells. His references to Jarry, as to Breton, Lautréamont, Duchamp, Lewis Carroll and William Burroughs, appearing in text, notes and elsewhere, suggest a varied inheritance of writers and artists whose experimentalism deliberately embraces the non-sensical. For many critics of the *avant-garde,* Surrealist and literary modernist traditions James Joyce is at the very centre of such experimentalism and, for some, the later work of Joyce represents an extreme locus of literary experimentalism in which the very possibility of making sense is indeed challenged. So it is not surprising to see him as a regular point of reference for Ballard. For most academic critics of Joyce, though, the texts do, at last potentially, make sense and I would argue that Ballard, even at his most extreme, depends upon this possibility too – and relies upon the Joycean precedent not only for experimental techniques but also for the possibility of them making sense.

Joyce was a figure of admiration and emulation for Ballard, if sometimes in an interestingly ambivalent way, and the legacy of an *avant-garde* Joyce is repeatedly felt in some of the most important forms and strategies of *The Atrocity Exhibition* which include several of its themes and motifs, its bold formal structures, its experimentation with character identities and psychologies and its extensive and labyrinthine intertextuality. Indeed the intertextual relation with Joyce is, I would suggest, deeper and more pervasive than the connection

---

3   See "Some Books from Ballard's Library" (*R/S JGB* 171), and the alphabetic "The Index" by Ballard to an "unpublished and perhaps suppressed autobiography" (*R/S JGB* 84–7), and in the oral compilation "From Shanghai to Shepperton" (*R/S JGB* 112–124). Much further useful information about Ballard's encounters with and attitudes to his "key influences" can be culled from scattered articles. Joyce appears in the "The Index" (*R/S JGB* 256) and in a gloss on the 1956 *New Worlds* profile note (*R/S JGB* 118–9).

with Jarry outlined above. Indeed it is the precedent of Joycean textuality with all of its challenges which makes it possible for the reader to embark on the novel with a context for its experimentalism and at the same time with the confidence that its experiments will be readable, even if not in a straightforward, common-sense way.

Joyce is not name-checked by Ballard in *The Atrocity Exhibition* nor in his notes (nor by William Burroughs in his introduction) but, when it came to the "revised, annotated and expanded" edition produced by Re/Search Publications in 1990, the Vale and Juno preface connects Ballardian textuality to that of Joyce, writing that "not since James Joyce ... has the novel form... been so illuminative of the shifting inner landscapes of its characters" (6). They go on to quote Ballard himself as he glosses that landscape in literary terms: "Its landscape is compounded of an enormous number of fictions, the fragments of the dream machine that produces our lifestyle right now. I mean fictions like TV, radio, politics, the press and advertising. Life is an enormous novel" (6). This "enormous novel" is clearly not the kind of realist novel said to be "exhausted" (*AE* 139) in *The Atrocity Exhibition* but more like the expansive multidimensional later novels of Joyce, which are precisely themselves built out of many previous novels as well as other texts from across the cultural sphere and beyond.[4] The Joycean presence may not ultimately dominate the Ballardian world as much as it does, for example, those of such near contemporaries as the experimental novelist B.S. Johnson (1933–1993) who was well known for his celebration of Joyce (*Aren't you Rather Young to be Writing your Memoirs?* in Bradbury 151–168), or the more mainstream novelist Anthony Burgess who wrote two books on Joyce.[5] Yet it is a fascinating and crucial one.

Joyce is acknowledged elsewhere in Ballard's writing frequently enough for us to get a sense of his importance to him. Mike Bonsall's Concordance counts it 18 times in the works (and "Joyce's" a further 8), mostly pointing the reader to essays in *User's Guide to the Millennium* and to references in *Miracles of Life* ("J.G. Ballard: The Concordance"). These include the 1990 *Guardian* tribute which begins "James Joyce had an immense influence on me," praises Joyce's "heroic modernism" and seems to highlight two significant moments in Ballard's reading of *Ulysses*: the first when he was an 18-year-old studying

---

4   My citations refer to episode and line numbers from the Hans Walter Gabler edition of *Ulysses*. Ballard would most likely have known *Ulysses* in the editions published by the Bodley Head in the UK from 1937 which included an extensive appendix including material from the American *Ulysses* censorship trial.

5   Anthony Burgess's work on Joyce included *Here Comes Everybody: An Introduction to James Joyce for the Ordinary Reader*, *The Shorter* Finnegans Wake, and *Joysprick: An Introduction to the Language of James Joyce*.

medicine at Cambridge after the war, which convinced him "to give up medicine and become a writer," and the second in the later 1980s (the period of the much-publicized Joyce centenary and Hans Gabler edition) when he was "even more impressed than I was forty years ago" (UGM 145). Yet, as a writer's model, Ballard explains, "*Ulysses* overwhelmed me," a formula repeated in his 1992 essay for Antonia Fraser's *The Pleasure of Reading* a couple of years later (when an early reading "in the sixth form" is recorded, UGM 181) and also in the account of his intellectual development that is given in *Miracles of Life* (ML 133, 149–50, 161). The familiar narrative confirmed in these places is that Ballard was much Joyce-inspired in his formative years as a writer but needed to find other models when establishing his own vision and voice.

Even when some of these comments on Joyce seem merely occasional, they can still help us chart the vital relationship between the two. Occasionally they play that relationship down. In his 1993 note, "Kafka in the Present Day," Ballard begins with Joyce but then goes on to claim that Kafka is "far more important than James Joyce" (UGM 146). In the 1971 essay "Fictions of Every Kind" Ballard praises the "compassion, lucidity and vision" of H.G. Wells over "the alienated and introverted fantasies" of modernists including Joyce (UGM 205). Such comments suggest his need to depart from a model of narrated interiority which he associates with Joyce, notwithstanding the fact that in Ballardian "inner space," "alienated and introverted fantasies" are very much in evidence. In *Kindness of Women* he writes that "Gray's *Anatomy* is a far greater novel than *Ulysses*" (KW 95). Such a blurring of the factual and fictional and critique of the novel in relation to medical science is apparently here made at Joyce's expense though, not untypically, it is something that readers of Joyce would recognize as a feature that Joyce himself (who called his novel an "encyclopaedia of the body") could be said to anticipate. Joyce, like Ballard, spent some time studying medicine before turning to writing fiction and, like Ballard, applies that experience and knowledge extensively in his work, using a different organ of the body to structure each of the 18 episodes of *Ulysses*. This famous feature of his book significantly prefigures Ballard's own use of vertebral or "spinal" sections as an anatomical metaphor for literary structure in *The Atrocity Exhibition*. Few would agree with Ballard's claim, in a 1991 review, that Molly Bloom's soliloquy could have seemed "contrived and mannered" by comparison with Henry Miller (UGM 111). There may be something of Molly Bloom's down-to-earth emotional honesty and humanity in the "kindness" of Ballard's women and Ballard himself surely acknowledges the legacy of the final "yes" of her soliloquy in the "existential yes" of *The Atrocity Exhibition* (AE 51). It is important to remember quite how closely associated with Surrealist Paris (and indeed Dadaist Zurich and Futurist Trieste) Joyce was. Even an extreme text such as Lautréamont's *Maldoror* (which Ballard quotes in *Atrocity*, AE 49 and "The Coming of the

Unconscious" review, *UGM* 85, calling it the "black bible of surrealism" in his review of books about Edward James, *UGM* 70), touches Joyce. Extracts from it in translation were first serialized in *The Egoist* magazine alongside Joyce's *A Portrait of the Artist as a Young Man,* without whose sensitive young quasi-autobiographical protagonist Stephen Dedalus, the Jim of *Empire of the Sun* would hardly have been possible.

The reader may well begin to gain the impression from much of this that, for all Ballard's ambivalence, Joyce is for him the pre-eminent experimental literary author, whose achievement is so secure and whose example so present that the main need of the younger writer is to attempt to downplay it to find space for their own imagination to grow. Joyce's own struggles as a writer, his difficulties with both censorship and exile, are not so much forgotten as they are taken as read as precedents for a Ballard, who found himself unable to publish *The Atrocity Exhibition* in America. In the 1960s Bill Butler, owner of an alternative bookshop in Brighton tried to publish "Why I Want to Fuck Ronald Reagan" as a separate pamphlet, and was charged with publishing obscenity just as Joyce's publishers feared they would be from *Dubliners* to *Ulysses.*

Even when apparently incidental, Ballard's references to Joyce can be striking and profound. One of the most remarkable of them appears in his review of the controversial translation of Hitler's *Mein Kampf,* which appeared in 1969 (*UGM* 223). Ballard comments that the most unnerving thing about reading *Mein Kampf* was that it humanized Hitler or at least made him somehow symptomatic as "one of the rightful inheritors of the twentieth century – the epitome of the half-educated man." He defines this humanity and its media landscape through Joyce's *Ulysses*:

> Wandering around the streets of Vienna shortly before the First World War, his head full of vague artistic yearnings and clap-trap picked up from popular magazines, whom does he most closely resemble? Above all, Leopold Bloom, his ostensible arch-enemy, wandering about Joyce's Dublin at about the same time, his head filled with the same clap-trap and the same yearnings. Both are children of the reference library and the self-improvement manual, of mass newspapers creating a new vocabulary of violence and sensation.
>
> *UGM* 223

For Ballard, then, Joyce's Bloom, was the embodiment of the modern everyman of the modern media landscape he had himself been defining in *The Atrocity Exhibition,* of which the fascist dictator was an opposite kind of symptom. We might be tempted to see Ballard sketching out here a profound reading of Bloom that is both Joycean and Kafka-esque, and which seems to prefigure the critique of the potential everyday fascism of consumer society that becomes increasingly prominent in his own later work up to and including *Kingdom Come* (2006). Joyce's Bloom is now celebrated by Joyce critics such as Garry Leonard, Jonathan Goldman or cultural theorists such as Michel de Certeau as one of the first fictional characters in whose consciousness the life of the streets, shopping and the awareness of consumer commodities all form important parts. That Ballard's writing is allied to this critical urban tradition, being for many its most important contemporary English manifestation, also seems clear.

It is fascinating to recognize the importance of Joyce's Bloom in defining the forms of modern consciousness that many of Ballard's protagonists share in these general terms. A further special affinity arises between Joyce's Bloom and Ballard because both work in the field of advertising. Bloom is a canvasser for a Dublin newspaper and Ballard, after a brief period studying English at Queen Mary College in London in 1951, gained a job "as a novice copywriter with a small London agency," "through a Cambridge friend in Benson's" (*ML* 153).[6] As Rick McGrath and John Baxter have suggested, it may well have been this experience that inspired the range of creative explorations and theories of advertising in Ballard's subsequent work. Ballard's name-sake in *Crash* works in advertising, as does Richard Pearson in the final novel, *Kingdom Come* (2006), which takes the critique of consumerism furthest of all (McGrath "What exactly is he trying to sell?"). Ballard's comment confirms that he sensed the importance of Joyce's advertising man Bloom in these terms.

In *Dubliners* Joyce had, like Ballard, written short stories which helped define the modern social world and, like Ballard's stories, they could be said to form parts of a larger fictional whole. Both writers could retain the episodic within the novelistic, Joyce retaining in all his longer works a strong episodic element which, makes them, like *The Atrocity Exhibition*, sit somewhere between a collection of stories and a novel. In *A Portrait of the Artist as a Young Man* he had written one of the most interesting autobiographies of the age and one which, like Ballard's *Empire of the Sun* and subsequent autobiographical writing, often subtly plays with the factual and fictional dimensions of the autobiographical genre.

It is however the ambitiously formal and experimental later Joyce, who is felt most significantly of all in *The Atrocity Exhibition*, for, whilst some aspects

---

6   As McGrath notes, that agency was not Benson's itself but Digby Wills, who advertised PLJ lemonade ("What exactly is he trying to sell?" and Baxter, *The Inner Man* 57–8, 169–70).

of the Joycean model (such as extended interior monologue) may not have been quite to Ballard's purpose, several others, such as structural discontinuity, sectionalization of the text with sub-headings, a discontinuous narrative protagonist, complex discursive layering and dense intertextual mosaic were absolutely central to it, forming, most properly, the stronger parts of its merger of Kafka, Joyce and Wells.

Joyce, like, Ballard, was inspired by the *avant-garde* energies of writers such as Marinetti, Tzara and Apollinaire who advocated a visible display of typographical experiment along with verbal play in their works. For many critics of Joyce's *Ulysses*, the clearest evidence of this influence occurs in the 7th or "Aeolus" episode, which is set in a newspaper office and whose narrative is interrupted every few paragraphs by bold-face newspaper-style headlines, which variously work to announce its content, pick out a memorable or distinctive word or phrase, embed its language in the everyday media landscape of the daily newspaper and work to produce an increasingly inebriated metacommentary on the action from a point of view which is neither that of the narrator, nor of any of the characters present. The "genetic" school of criticism in the 1970s and 80s revealed that Joyce added this feature of "Aeolus" late in the composition process of the book and this clearly announces it as an *avant-garde* narrative, in which stylistic play takes off or, as Karen Lawrence has argued, can even take over from represented content (74).

Joyce-aware readers of *The Atrocity Exhibition* (whose presence Ballard acknowledges among modern readers of science-fiction as well as amongst academics) will instantly recognize this as a point of kinship between the two texts (*ML* 195). The fifteen sections of Ballard's book are further subdivided into sub-sections, bearing single words or phrases in bold face. These might in some cases highlight their content or terminology, in other cases produce a network of interconnections between them and in yet other cases make allusions to the intertextual points of reference in the media landscape analyzed above. Ballard had used section headings in earlier stories such as *Atrocity*'s precursor story "The Terminal Beach" but here they become far more important (Pringle "You and Me and the Continuum"). In one unnerving development Ballard's subsection headings are repeated in chapter headings and then repeated again in the various alternative titles under which the text was published in whole or in parts. In one of the most interesting developments from a narratorial and structural point of view, the headings switch radically in their function from the end of Chapter 9. In Chapters 10, 11, 12 and 14 they become parts of continuous sentences of which the T-figure, who has disappeared from the narrative proper, becomes the subject (Tallis in 10, 12 and 14; Traven in 11). This shifts the plane of representation, producing an alternative geometry of reading, reality and feeling, with these brief mini-narratives headlining sections in the parody analytic report style. Such a deliberately asymmetrical structuring device may appear, to many readers, to be close to being no structure at all. However, it will be recognizable to a reader of Joyce's "Aeolus" episode where the headlines sometimes play similar tricks. The strategy is especially powerful here as it seems to open up another significant dimension of Ballard's text.

In the first of these section-headline narratives in Chapter 10 Tallis is obsessed with images of Jacqueline Kennedy who seems to have the power to "summon to her side all the legions of the bereaved" (AE 133). In Chapter 11 it is the spectre of Traven's daughter's body who "summoned to her side all the legions of the bereaved" (AE 150) and in Chapter 11 Tallis recognizes the endless images of car crashes, as "celebrations" of his wife's death. Inevitably this calls to mind not just the abstracted geometry of juxtaposed forms that underpins the pseudo-logic of the text and its apocalyptic critique of celebrity culture but also the intense personal bereavement felt by Ballard himself for his wife Mary, mother of their three children, who had died suddenly in Alicante in 1964 only a year before the first of the stories that went into *The Atrocity Exhibition* began to appear. The autobiographical became an increasingly prominent part of Ballard's writing and the intensity of that loss became more apparent. Mary is beautifully recalled in the "magic world" of *The Kindness of Women* and in *Miracles of Life*. The personal impact of her death on the strange obsessive fantasies of assassination that went into *The Atrocity Exhibition*, here seems no less profound. It is no wonder, then, that recent readings of Ballard by Sam Francis, Emma Whiting and Jen Hui Bon Hua have begun to explore the complex sexual psychologies of trauma, abjection and the therapeutic in the text in highly promising and productive ways (Francis 95–107; Whiting 88–104; Hui Bon Hua 71–87).[7] If we can accept that *The Atrocity Exhibition* subtly fuses such personal and public material it may be especially interesting to note that it does so at a stylistic level by merging the headlines of the "Aeolus" episode with some of the Surrealism of the "Circe" or "nighttown" episode of *Ulysses*.

Another prominent stylistic feature of *Atrocity*, perhaps the most prominent of them, further confirms its deep imaginative and technical kinship with James Joyce: that is the transforming or modular identity of the protagonist, Traven, Travis and his seven names, who I have referred to as the T-figure above, and who Roger Luckhurst calls the T-Cell (86). In Ballard's authorial note to "You and Me and the Continuum" (AE 138) he glosses the central protagonist's

---

7 Emma Whiting argues that the passage into Ballardian "inner space" may have "redemptive and therapeutic power" (88).

subjectivity as "a succession of roles" or "spectrum of possibilities" which are "available to each of us in our interior lives." In this section, he is, he says, "at his most apocalyptic, appearing as the second coming of Christ" (*AE* 138).

In the "Oxen of the Sun" episode of *Ulysses* Joyce narrates his maternity hospital scene in a succession of prose styles which pastiche the history of English prose and the names of the characters are transformed at different stages there into versions appropriate to these different styles. Identities are rendered unstable in other ways in *Ulysses* too, not least in the theory of Shakespeare propounded by Stephen Dedalus, according to which we have the theatrical sense that actors can be transformed into Shakespeare's characters but also that these characters can themselves be understood as transformations of the "spectrum of possibilities" of the author's own core identity.

In Joyce's *Finnegans Wake* this experiment with composite identity is vastly extended, creating a fictional world where names and identities are in a continual state of merging and transformation often marked by the verbal similarities between them. The main protagonist of the book, variously named Harold or Humphrey Chimpden Earwicker, or "Here Comes Everybody," is typical in that his presence or identity at any point in the text is most frequently marked by the presence of the initial letters of these forms of his name: "h," "c" and "e." In his 1964 *New Worlds* review of *The Naked Lunch* Ballard is fulsome in his enthusiasm for *Finnegans Wake* (*UGM* 126,129), which went back to his school-days in Cambridge. Whilst this subsequently becomes the text from which he has to declare his independence, readers of the later Joyce will have little difficulty in recognizing its legacy in the multiple identity of Ballard's protagonist and in the shifting levels of textuality in his *avant-garde* narrative technique. The three mysterious characters or presences, Xero, Coma and Kline, who appear to form part of the surveillance of the T-figure but merge, for instance, into billboards of Jackie Kennedy, Lee Harvey Oswald and Malcolm X, might appear as developments of the handling of characterization in *Finnegans Wake*, explicitly recognised in his account of the book in the Burroughs review when he writes:

> In *Finnegans Wake,* a gigantic glutinous pun, James Joyce brought the novel up to date, circa 1940, with his vast cyclical dream-rebus of a Dublin publican who is simultaneously Adam, Napoleon and the heroes of a thousand mythologies.
>
> *UGM* 126

Finnegans Wake informs the fascinating intertextual nexus that seems to link the long genesis of *The Atrocity Exhibition* to the four spreads of the poster-style

Project for a New Novel, one of Ballard's boldest experiments from the 1950s in writing and visual form and reprinted by Luckhurst, Baxter, the Vale publications and elsewhere. David Pringle's ingenious sleuthing in an article which was subsequently corrected and partly confirmed by Ballard himself makes the *Project for a New Novel* contemporary with a possible earlier version of his "botched second coming" story or section "You and Me and the Continuum" (Pringle "You and Me and the Continuum"). The words and phrases of Ballard's text accompanying extracts from scientific journalism are transcribed in Pringle's article and he points to some of their subsequent use in various stories, as well as sections of *The Atrocity Exhibition*. Ballard's note confirms that, in addition to these few phrases, he had "written about 50–60 pages of an experimental novel," to which he added "until I had a totally unpublishable farrago of apocalyptic material."

Even if they are not all he meant by it, these pages presumably reflect Ballard's earlier rejected attempt to write like Joyce and to describe that as part of his "apocalyptic" vision. The December 1956 *New Worlds* profile, cited by Pringle and acknowledged by Ballard as self-authored, confirms as much: "After winning the annual short story competition at Cambridge in 1951 he wrote his first novel, a completely unreadable pastiche of *Finnegans Wake* and *The Adventures of Engelbrecht*. James Joyce still remains the wordmaster, but it wasn't until he turned to science fiction that he found a medium where he could exploit his imagination, being less concerned with the popular scientific approach than using it as a springboard into the surreal and fantastic" (Luckhurst 86).

We can observe in *Project for a New Novel* the presence of newspaper-style headlines, reminiscent of Marinetti, Apollinaire, Wyndham Lewis and especially of Joyce, and several other elements which may link Ballard's experiments not only to the Joycean idea but to the texts of Joyce. The first is the phrase "beach Hamlet," which (especially in its *Project* form "am: beach hamlet") will instantly resonate with readers of *Ulysses* in relation to Joyce's intellectual figure Stephen Dedalus, who plays a number of intertextual roles in *Ulysses*, including that of Telemachus to Bloom's Odysseus and that of Prince Hamlet. Stephen theorizes about Hamlet all through the book's day, not least during the morning in the third or "Proteus" episode. This sees him in interior monologue, walking from the history lesson he has just taught, along the beach in Dublin into the centre of town and engaging in a flood of melancholic speculations about his mother's death and his cultural usurpation that make him such a strong analogy for Hamlet even without the patterns of allusion that confirm the link, such as the phrase "A side eye at my Hamlet hat" that occurs here (*U* 3. 340).

Ballard's phrase "am: beach hamlet" which could fit several of the protagonists of his fiction from *Terminal Beach* to *Super-Cannes*, may well be a memory of or even gloss on Joyce's Stephen Dedalus in *Ulysses* and is therefore mediated by Joyce, as also are the other two Shakespearean references mentioned above. Caliban is a Shakespeare character but it is in the preface to Oscar Wilde's *The Picture of Dorian Gray* that he is construed as a figure angry at his own reflection and, in the development of this image in Joyce's *Ulysses*, that this reflection is literally a mirror. Stephen's well-known image of Irish art as a cracked looking-glass prefigures and is recalled in Ballard's more grotesque and chaotic image of human desperation.

A third reference – to Richard Burton and Elizabeth Taylor's Shakespearean roles – is a part of the Institute's proposed staging of them as Theseus and Ariadne in an "elegant" film version of the story of the minotaur in "The Great American Nude." This is apparently a dark and obsessive Ballardian version in which the studio set becomes a labyrinth, itself "an exact formalization of each curve and cleavage" of the body of the actress, where sex is a conceptual act bearing the name "Elizabeth" and intended as a form of conceptual death for her and/or for Karen Novotny. At the end of the section the "Daedalus in this neural drama" arrives, reminding us that Joyce took the name of his famous autobiographical persona Stephen Daedalus from the Cretan myth and that Joyce himself remains for many the prime example of the Dedalian or labyrinthine artist (*AE* 87). Stephen Dedalus was the fictional name Joyce famously selected for his own fictional alter-ego in both *A Portrait of the Artist as a Young Man* and *Ulysses* and the prominent critical discussions about the complicated relations of the autobiographical and the fictional in that process surely provided a platform upon which Ballard's no less extraordinary experiments in autobiographical fiction and autobiography, including James Ballard in *Crash*, followed by more clearly autobiographical personae in *Empire of the Sun*, *Kindness of Women*, and *Miracles of Life*, could be built.

No readers of Joyce, or even readers only passingly acquainted with *Ulysses* by hearsay, would fail to hear resonances between Molly's famously repeated "yes" of acceptance and affirmation at the end of the "Penelope" episode of *Ulysses* and Ballard's phrase "the existential yes," which is imported from the *Project* for a subsection title in the third section "The Assassination Weapon" as "An Existential Yes" (*AE* 51), along with other phrases and some extended narrative presence for the three mysterious characters Xero, Coma and Kline. If we return to the *Project* notes in the light of Joyce's *Ulysses*, we might recall that Leopold Bloom returns in the evening to the same beach which Stephen has visited in the morning where, in the "Nausicaa" episode, he meets limping Gerty McDowell, the imagined muse of his evening masturbation who might, translated back into Ballard's world, almost appear as an extraordinary prefiguration of the crash-wounded, scarred, crippled and fetishistic Gabrielle in *Crash*. The "Penelope" episode concludes the book with its "yes." Joyce's book is so definable by its three main characters that, conceivably, a microscopically "condensed novel" version of it in its three episodes "Proteus," "Nausicaa" and "Penelope" might be discerned in the "Spread 2" of Ballard's *Project* novel:

> am: beach hamlet
> pm: imago tapes
> : the existential yes!

The extract from the science journal "Fresh water from sea water is one way to relieve the shortage of both industrial and municipal water" will immediately remind readers of *Ulysses* of the long intervening 17th chapter "Ithaca," where extensive pseudo-scientific explanations of phenomena are given at length, including a famous account of the infrastructure of Dublin's municipal water supply, given when Leopold Bloom turns on the tap. The word "yes" is reprised and repeated "yes...yes...yes...yes" on the fourth spread of Ballard's *Project* as it is famously at the conclusion of *Ulysses* in the monologue of Molly Bloom, which Joyce described in one much-quoted letter as Bloom's indispensible "passport to eternity," that phrase, of course, also providing Ballard with the title of a short story (*CSS1* 461–481).

Ballard's reference to Joyce at one time as the "wordmaster," when at others he attempts to deny the Joycean influence, suggests a classic Harold Bloomian "anxiety of influence" where authorial denial of direct influence is the proof of influence of a deeply unconscious kind (Bloom 11). Joyce is the Oedipal father yet also at times an acknowledged Virgil to Ballard's Dante, leading him to a media landscape of modernity and an underworld of the Surrealistic and *avant-garde*, implying connections which are more conscious than unconscious and more subtle and complex than can be accounted for within Harold Bloom's strictly Oedipal frame. Where Ballard's writing takes from the Joycean example, it takes it in a direction of its own. According to Joyce-inspired contemporary B.S. Johnson, for writers of their generation, "It is not a question of influence, of writing like Joyce. It is a matter of realizing that the novel is an evolving form, not a static one, of accepting that for practical purposes where Joyce left off should ever since have been a starting point" (*Aren't You Rather Young* 12–13). Ballard's

Atrocity Exhibition is one of the few novels of the time which manages to do that.

We might chart many more points of detailed connection between Joyce and *The Atrocity Exhibition* let alone between Joyce and Ballard but need to return to the broader opening point about the apocalyptic intertextuality of Ballard's text. It would be misleading to argue that Joyce is the only key to *The Atrocity Exhibition* or that somehow everything apparently new in it had already been done by Joyce. It is far nearer the mark to say that Ballard's experimentalism revitalized and re-energised Joycean experimentation for a contemporary anglophone literary world in which it represented a high water mark of achievement which it would be difficult or impossible to surpass. Hence the strange mix of avowals and denials in Ballard's critical comments and accompanying claims that *The Atrocity Exhibition* offers a novelistic experiment in some ways matching or at least well worthy of comparison to Joyce.

Ballard's experiment did not need to name or acknowledge Joyce as an aspect of its represented world but does so profoundly in creating a modern consciousness which, like Bloom's, is immersed in a media landscape of consumerism, popular literature, journalistic media and popular science, a consciousness which, like the more extreme subjectivities in the later Joyce, may be discontinuous, fragmentary and traumatised, and perhaps only be fully representable through stylistic experiment.

Joyce is an intrinsic part of the apocalyptic intertextuality of Ballard's world and informs *The Atrocity Exhibition* not least because of the intertextuality of his own writing. Its complex and multi-dimensional allusiveness anticipates that of the later writer, establishing a precedent for complex textuality and for intertextual forms of reading which can offer the best ways to approach a text whose main stylistic features – programmatic asymmetry of characterization, location, plotting, levels of consciousness – all mitigate against conventional mimetic reading even where content may be at its most affectively charged, requiring instead to be read at the level of textual relations, forms and ideas.

The concluding section "The Assassination of John Fitzgerald Kennedy Considered as a Downhill Bicycle Race" is delightfully Jarry-esque, and the text involves a wealth of allusion to cultural texts that can similarly illuminate aspects of its multi-dimensional work. *The Atrocity Exhibition* as a whole has the variety, scope and ambition that invites and justifies an extended comparison with Ballard's early "wordmaster" James Joyce who can provide a rich guide to its intertextual labyrinth. Exploring the intertextuality of the Ballardian media landscape is among the most rewarding ways of exploring *The Atrocity Exhibition,* which is his most demanding text. By exploring that media landscape through Joyce we can rise to that demand and recognize the scale of the achievement all the more.

Works Cited

Bloom, Harold. *The Anxiety of Influence.* New York and Oxford: Oxford University Press, 1973.

Bradbury, Malcolm. Ed. *The Novel Today.* London: Fontana, 1977.

Burgess, Anthony. *Here Comes Everybody: An Introduction to James Joyce for the Ordinary Reader.* 1965.

Burgess, Anthony. *The Shorter* Finnegans Wake. London: Faber, 1969.

Burgess, Anthony. *Joysprick: An Introduction to the Language of James Joyce.* 1973.

De Certeau, Michel. *The Practice of Everyday Life.* Translated by *Stephen Rendall.* Berkeley: University of California Press, 1984.

Goldman, Jonathan. *Modernism is the Culture of Celebrity.* Austin: University of Texas Press, 2011.

Hui Bon Hua, Jen. "Pornographic Geometries: The Spectacle as Pathology and Therapy in *The Atrocity Exhibition.*" In *J.G. Ballard: Visions and Revisions.* Edited by Jeannette Baxter and Rowland Wymer. London: Palgrave Macmillan, 2012. 71–87.

Johnson, B.S. *Aren't you Rather Young to be Writing your Memoirs?* London: Hutchinson 1973.

Joyce, James. *Ulysses.* [1922]. Oxford: Oxford University Press: The World's Classics, 2000.

Joyce, James. *Ulysses.* [1922]. London: Penguin, 1984.

Joyce, James. *Finnegans Wake.* [1939]. Oxford: Oxford University Press: World's Classics, 2012.

Lawrence, Karen. *The Odyssey of Style in* Ulysses. Princeton: Princeton University Press, 1984.

Leonard, Garry. *Advertising and Commodity Culture in Joyce.* Gainesville: University of Florida Press, 1998.

McGrath, Rick. "'What exactly is he trying to sell?': J.G. Ballard's Adventures in Advertising." May 2009. Web. 5 August 2015.

Pringle, David. "You and Me and the Continuum: In Search of a Lost J.G. Ballard Novel." *Adventures Thru Inner Space: Essays and Articles.* 1993. Web. 12 September 2015. Roussel, Raymond. *Impressions of Africa* [1910]. Translated by Mark Polizzotti. Dublin: Dalkey Archive, 2011.

Roussel, Raymond. *Locus Solus* [1914]. London: Calder, 2008.

Shattuck, Roger and Simon Taylor. Eds. *Selected Works of Alfred Jarry.* New York: Grove Press, 1965.

Quin, Ann. *Berg*. London: Marion Boyars, 1964.

Quin, Ann. *Three*. London: Dalkey Archive Press, 2001.

Quin, Ann. *Passages*. London: Dalkey Archive Press, 2003.

Quin, Ann. *Tripticks*. London: Marion Boyars, 1972.

Warren E. "Report of the President's Commission on the Assassination of President Kennedy." Washington: United States Government Printing Office, 1964. The U.S. National Archives and Records Administration. Web. 5 August 2015.

Whiting, Emma. "Disaffection and Abjection in J.G. Ballard's *The Atrocity Exhibition* and *Crash*." In *J.G. Ballard: Visions and Revisions*. Edited by Jeannette Baxter and Rowland Wymer. London: Palgrave Macmillan, 2012. 88–104.

CHAPTER 6

Geometries of the Imagination: The Map-Territory Relation in *The Atrocity Exhibition*

Guglielmo Poli

Abstract

The chapter presents a reading of *The Atrocity Exhibition* (1970) as a reflection on human perception. An influence in Ballard's work, Alfred Korzybski defined the modalities of perception through the formula: "the map is not the territory." Asserting that human knowledge is determined by the nervous system and by the structure of language, Korzybski wanted to demonstrate intuitively how everyone's mental map, a construction for comprehending the reality that surrounds the individual, is only a mark of more complex phenomena. This essay demonstrates how Korzybski's formula and especially Gregory Bateson's interpretation are aligned with Ballard's poetics, synthesized in *The Atrocity Exhibition* in the image of Caliban and the mirror.

Keywords

J.G. Ballard – *The Atrocity Exhibition* – Alfred Korzybski – Gregory Bateson – inner space – perception – central nervous system – ontology – prochronism – Caliban

In this chapter I am going to interpret Ballard's *The Atrocity Exhibition* (1970) using the ideas expressed in the formula "the map is not the territory" (750), coined by the Polish thinker Alfred Korzybski and subsequently reused by the British anthropologist Gregory Bateson. The focus of my discussion will not be on the atrocities narrated in the book, but rather on *how*, through their narration, these atrocities have been observed and represented. My analysis will explore the blurred line that divides fiction (the map) and reality (the territory) as it is expressed in the book, to show how these two terms are, in Ballard's work, often interchangeable. Bateson's interpretation of Korzybski's formula, I argue, gives clues to an understanding of what Ballard has defined as "inner space": "that psychological domain (manifest, for example, in surrealist painting) where the inner world of the mind and the outer world of reality meet and fuse" (*R/SJGB* 97).

The Atrocity Exhibition is a book that, through the perspective of the insane mind, gives us the keys to interpret what sanity is. In Ballard's clinic, patients and doctors are indistinguishable, *"was my husband a doctor, or a patient?"* Mrs Travis asks (AE 6). Here, the visual sphere is fundamental. For the psychoanalyst and the neurologist, the patient's body is the theatre in which the symptoms of a disturbed relation with reality are staged in a ciphered way. At the same time, in the eyes of patients, these symptoms spread into the external surroundings because their reality is affected by their mental disorders. This is clear, for instance, in the following passage where Dr Nathan explains that for Travis: "The blitzkriegs will be fought out on the spinal battlefields, in terms of the postures we assume, of our traumas mimetized in the angle of a wall or balcony" (AE 7). This is one of the ways in which the body in *The Atrocity Exhibition* is exteriorized. Through a "dialectic of contraries" Ballard, in the main character of *The Atrocity Exhibition* converts the patient into a doctor, constructing a fascinating proposition. If texts written by psychoanalysts in full possession of their mental capacities are used to understand an insane reality, then the text of an insane doctor might be used to understand what appears as a sane reality. Hence, human perception is the major theme of the novel and, as the end of the section "The Lost Symmetry of the Blastosphere" puts it, the atrocity exhibition is the human organism of which the characters are "unwilling spectators" (AE 9).

In the aseptic language of Ballard's book, borrowed from the medical lexicon of the scientific journals, one recognizes a constant emphasis on the *forms* rather than on the *substance* of the narrated objects and phenomena, an insistence on a methodology rather than on a mere description. The narrative's elements are divested of their emotive connotations and functional nature, while the characters, together with their surroundings, are part of a "geometric pattern" (AE 11) or "mysterious equation" (AE 62), which is revealed through their eyes. An obsessive search for meaning moves these characters who want to explore the nature of the relations between themselves and the landscape: "These matters involve a *relativity* of a very different kind" (emphasis mine) (AE 6), Nathan, the presumed doctor, says to Catherine Austin, the wife of at least one of the embodiments of the T-character, Travis. In fact, all of *The Atrocity Exhibition* is pervaded by a relativism different from the common definition (the *cultural* one), but found in the etymological meaning of "relation" (from the Latin *relatus*, "to relate"): a superstructure with its mysterious geometry in which the individual acts essentially by virtue of the relations decreed by his or her own perception of reality. At the base of these concepts there is the central nervous system, the means by which human beings experience the world and, undoubtedly, one of the main protagonists of *The Atrocity Exhibition*. This will be defined by a more mature Ballard in *The Kindness of Women* (1991) as "nature's Sistine Chapel" (KW 166), confirming the thesis that "the world our senses present to us is a ramshackle construct which our brains have devised to let us get on with the job of maintaining ourselves and reproducing our species. What we see is a highly conventionalised picture, a simple tourist guide to a very strange city" (*KW* 166).

The following annotation by Ballard accompanying the fragment "Suite Mentale," is particularly revealing in light of this line of analysis:

> The paintings of mental patients, like those of the surrealists, show remarkable insights into our notions of *conventional reality, a largely artificial construct which serves the limited ambitions of our central nervous systems*. Huge arrays of dampers suppress those perceptions that confuse or unsettle the central nervous system, and if these are bypassed, most dramatically by LSD, startling revelations soon begin to occur. [...] Some of these *transformational grammars* I have tried to decode in the present book. [...] The characters behave as if they were pieces of geometry interlocking in a series of mysterious equations [emphasis mine].
>
> *AE* 62

Ballard's observations bear a close resemblance to the theories of the Polish mathematician and philosopher Alfred Korzybski, whose ideas were synthesized in the formula "the map is not the territory" (750).[1] Korzybski suggests that our senses are able to conceive reality, but only in a partial way, because our minds are susceptible to distortions, generalizations and cancellations. Korzybski went on to maintain that human knowledge of the world is limited by the nervous system and by the structure of language. According to him, men do not have direct access to the knowledge of reality, but rather to their perceptions and to a set of beliefs that human society has confused with the direct access to reality. For this reason Korzybski theorized the metaphor of the mental map that everyone constructs to comprehend outer reality but which is, in fact, only the mark of more complex phenomena: "If we use languages of a structure non-similar to the world and our nervous system, our verbal predictions are not verified empirically, we cannot be 'rational' or adjusted" (751).

As Simon Sellars has pointed out (55–56), Ballard was aware of Korzybski's ideas, and they manifest themselves in the following passage from *Empire of the Sun* (1984). About to leave Shanghai, the young protagonist Jim, pretends to know where Woosung is (the place of "the welcoming world of the prison camps," 2008: 126), and earns the seat next to the soldier who, without a map, is

---

1   Korzybski was also the teacher of a twenty-five-years-old William Burroughs who went to Chicago to attend his lessons (Morgan 71–73).

driving the van bringing the Western prisoners towards the internment zone. Unsurprisingly perhaps, Jim gives the wrong directions, the convoy gets lost and, while the Japanese soldier swears at the wheel, Jim holds a conversation with a British official in the back who asks him if they are lost. Jim then answers:

> 'Not really. They just haven't captured any maps.'
> 'Good – *never confuse the map with the territory* [...]' [emphasis mine]
>   ES 129

Another direct reference to the Korzybski sentence appears in *The Atrocity Exhibition* in the annotation to the fragment "Plan for the Assassination of Jacqueline Kennedy": "The media landscape of the present day is a map in search of a territory" (*AE* 145).

The scientist who made Korzybski's formula famous in the second part of the twentieth century was the British anthropologist Gregory Bateson. In the lecture entitled *Form, Substance and Difference* (*Ecology of Mind* 453–471) held on the 9th of January 1970 on the occasion of the Annual Korzybski Memorial, Bateson largely focused on the definition of the relations between the organism and the environment and, in particular, on the inadequate capacity of the human race to think the boundaries of these relations. Recalling the formula "the map is not the territory," Bateson shows that everything in our culture consists of names, maps and names of relations, but the name of a thing is never that thing, as a map never corresponds perfectly with the territory that it aims to represent. Bateson criticizes the illusory objectivity upon which our knowledge is based: the external world is not made up of objects, by the Kantian *Ding an Sich*,[2] the thing-in-itself. For Bateson, and indeed Ballard, the external world is made up by our perceptions of the differences. Bateson uses an example to better define what a difference is. If we take a piece of paper and a wooden table, we see that the piece of paper is different from the wooden table. But where is the difference? Obviously it is not *in* the paper and not even *in* the table. It is not in the space between them, nor in the time between them (which is what we call "change"). A difference, then, is an abstract matter. Differences are not "things," but the product of the transformation of paired or multiple events, and Bateson uses the word "transforms" (*Ecology of Mind* 460) in which they are immanent but not localizable; so, differences are abstract matters. Recalling Korzybski's aphorism "the map is not the territory,"

---

2 Blackburn explains that in "Kantian metaphysics the thing in itself exists independently of us, unfiltered by the forms of sense. It is not in space or time, and cannot be known" (*Oxford Dictionary of Philosophy* 101).

Bateson explains that the thing-in-itself, Korzybski's territory, is excluded from the representational process by the difference. What we see and perceive is the representation built up by our mind. The mental world is built up by maps, but the true reality, or the "valid reality" (AE 72), is hidden from us by the difference. Therefore, our mind does not contain things, but pieces of information about things. Consequently, what we see and perceive is the map of a thing, the world of commonsense, which is the one studied by the hard sciences. What Bateson illustrates instead is a "world of communication [...] a world in which 'effects' [...] are brought about by *differences*. That is, they are brought about by the sort of 'thing' that gets onto the map from the territory. This is difference" (*Ecology of Mind* 458).

According to Bateson, not only is the map not the territory, but the rules of transformation used to make a map, which allow the reader to comprehend it, are not the map either. What has been defined up to this point as difference stands also as a synonym for the word idea. This is because there are an infinite number of differences around and within the *Ding an Sich*, and of this infinitude we select only a definite number, which is information. Our brain's processing of this information is, in turn, a "*difference which makes a difference*" (*Ecology of Mind* 459), which is another way of saying, an idea. In the corner of every serious map there are the rules of its codifications, for instance, the linear scale or the map colouring, that allow the reader to understand it. The processing in our brain of these codifications is "a difference of a difference," information that changes a mind-system, a "news of a difference" or a *message* (*Ecology of Mind* 459–460).

Borrowing from Jung the Gnostic notions of *pleroma* and *creatura*, Bateson shows how these pieces of information operate in the pathways outside and inside the body. The *pleromatic* is the world governed by forces and impacts, in which there are no differences; on the other hand, in the *creatural* the effects are triggered precisely by the differences. Therefore, *creatura* is the mental world and it is an error to think about it as being contained inside the body's frame:

> The individual mind is immanent but not only in the body. It is immanent also in pathways and messages outside the body; and there is a larger Mind of which the individual mind is only a subsystem. This larger Mind is comparable to God and is perhaps what some people mean by "God," but it is still immanent in the total interconnected social system and planetary ecology.

Freudian psychology expanded the concept of mind inwards to include the whole communication system within the body – the autonomic, the

habitual, and the vast range of unconscious process. What I am saying
expands mind outwards. And both of these changes reduce the scope of
the conscious self.

Ecology of the Mind 467

What Bateson is proposing here is a world built up by relations, where to be
is to be related. If this is to be accepted, we can draw at least two conclusions.
Firstly, emotions are a *consistent* part of the physical world since memories
are the relevant parts of an individual mind. Twenty-five years before the
groundbreaking book by Antonio Damasio, *Descartes' Error* (1994) Bateson expressed more or less the same ideas: "It is the attempt to separate intellect from
emotion that is monstrous, and I suggest that it is equally monstrous – and
dangerous – to attempt to separate the external mind from the internal. Or to
separate mind from body" (*Ecology of the Mind* 470).

If the internal mind is outside the boundaries of the body, then emotions
are also a consistent part of the external world. Bateson depicts an identity
between the unit of evolutionary survival and the unit of mind. The mind,
Bateson says, like nature, is partitive. The units of evolution are, at every step,
to be considered as organisms together with the complete pathways outside
them, namely an environment. On the other hand, mind is composed by a hierarchy of sub-systems, any one of which we can call an individual mind. The
two systems operate in the same way and "each step of the hierarchy is to be
thought of as a system, instead of a chunk cut off and visualized as against
the surrounding matrix. This identity between the unit of mind and the unit
of evolutionary survival is of very great importance, not only theoretical, but
also ethical. It means, you see, that [...] mind is immanent in the total evolutionary structure" (*Ecology of the Mind* 466). Thus, Bateson theorizes a sort
of mental determinism, a world where the *creatura* is more significant than
the *pleroma*: "[Bateson] sees life and mind as coexisting in an ecological and
evolutionary dynamic that integrates the whole biosphere" (Brier 97).

As Dan O'Hara has pointed out ("Reading Posture and Gesture," 108), we do
not know if Ballard read Bateson's articles and books, but it is possible to as-
sert that both Bateson and Ballard observed the physical world from the same
perspective. In fact, for both of them, the external physical world cannot be
thought of as something separated from the internal mental world; the two are
interconnected, and the way in which the pieces of information are transmit-
ted between them is very important. Ballard uses the category of inner space to
describe the psychological domain where the inner world of the mind and the
outer world of reality meet and fuse. Meanwhile, Bateson suggests that, in order
to deepen our comprehension of these connections, non-familiar languages

should be used, such as those of poets, artists and insane people.[3] Largely escaping the common binary logic of our brain, these systems of representation have a better grasp on the relation between the map and the territory. These are precisely the languages Ballard uses in *The Atrocity Exhibition* because only these languages of art, dream and imagination are really able to offer a sense of unity between mind and nature. This is not because art, dreams or madness are pure forms of expression of the unconscious, but because they are able to bring into relation the different levels that are traditionally disjointed, such as form and substance, body and mind, concreteness and imagination.

An analysis of this substantial passage may help us to see this perception at work in Ballard's text:

> **The Lost Symmetry of the Blastosphere**. 'This reluctance to accept the fact of his own consciousness,' Dr Nathan wrote, 'may reflect certain positional difficulties in the immediate context of time and space. The right-angle spiral of a stairwell may remind him of similar biases within the chemistry of the biological kingdom. This can be carried to remarkable lengths – for example, the jutting balconies of the Hilton Hotel have become identified with the lost gill-slits of the dying film actress, Elizabeth Taylor. Much of Travis's thought concerns what he terms "the lost symmetry of the blastosphere" – the primitive precursor of the embryo that is the last structure to preserve perfect symmetry in all planes. It occurred to Travis that our own bodies may conceal the rudiments of a symmetry not only about the vertical axis but also the horizontal. [...] it seems that Travis's extreme sensitivity to the volumes and geometry of the world around him, and their immediate translation into psychological terms, may reflect a belated attempt to return to a symmetrical world, one that will recapture the perfect symmetry of the blastosphere, and the acceptance of the "Mythology of the Amniotic Return". In his mind World War III represents the final self-destruction and imbalance of an asymmetric world. The human organism is an atrocity exhibition at which he is an unwilling spectator ...'
>
> AE 8–9

If *The Atrocity Exhibition* is, as Colin Greenland has argued, "a minimal overlay of narrative gestures on a mass of theory" (115), then this paragraph contains

---

3   This acknowledges the respect that Ballard had for the insane: "I imagine my mental patients conflating Freud and Liz Taylor in their Warhol-like efforts, unerringly homing in on the first signs of their doctor's nervous breakdown. *The Atrocity Exhibition*'s original dedication should have been 'To the Insane'. I owe them everything" (AE 14).

considerable clues to the mass of theory behind it. First of all, the hierarchy of the biological organization is identified with the mental projections of Travis. This is clear, for instance, in the recognition of an equivalence between the jutting balconies of the Hilton Hotel and the "lost gill-slits" of Elizabeth Taylor. We know from Ballard's annotation to the 1990 edition of *The Atrocity Exhibition* that the actress "was staying at the Hilton during the shooting of *Cleopatra*, when she contracted pneumonia and was given a tracheotomy. The Hilton's balconies remind Travis of the actress's lost gill-slits" (*AE* 16). The "prochronism," i.e. "the general truth that organisms carry, in their forms, evidences of their past growth" (Bateson *Mind and Nature* 230), of the actress is identified by Travis with the hotel's architecture as well as with his memories. This is because the collective memory determined by the media landscape, as Ballard calls it,[4] is what produces such memories. Travis' search for a meaning through his extreme sensitivity to the world solves a problem in the formation of a pattern in which he is able to discern the lineage which connects the actress, and the entire human race, to the ancestral fish. Travis *sees* (or perceives) what Bateson calls "the pattern which connects" (*Mind and Nature* 8), which is the mental determinism we have discussed above. Subsequently, he traces horizontal analogies that link the hierarchical levels of the biological kingdom to the ones of the mind, showing the "affiliation under that pattern of patterns which connect" (*Mind and Nature* 12). Finally, he conceives of World War III as a loss of symmetry, an imbalance. In fact, if everything has to be organized through analogies, as a world built up only by relations (as Travis feels it), then a rupture of this pattern is what brings him to a crisis.[5] For Travis, World War III is the terminal catastrophe caused by the collapse of the pattern which connects: a superstructure that expresses the unity of the natural world through its constitutive formal relations. "The Lost Symmetry of the Blastosphere" passage shows a world view where ontogeny coincides with phylogeny. Ballard applies the *creatural* over the *pleromatic* world, the world of the mind over the world of the commonsense.

For Bateson, this *creatural* world has another constitutive element which he calls stories. Lingering, like Ballard, on "the embryo, symbol of secret growth and possibility" (*AE* 24), he writes,

---

4   Ballard uses the term "media landscape" nineteen times in the interviews collected in *Extreme Metaphors* (2012).

5   It should be noted that George L. Mosse pinpoints exactly the historical roots of racism in the strangers' lack of symmetry of the ancient Greek's model of beauty, as it was reconsidered during the 18th century in Europe (10–15).

[...] if the world be connected, if I am at all fundamentally right in what I am saying, then *thinking in terms of stories* must be shared by all mind or minds, whether ours or those of redwood forests and sea anemones.

Context and relevance must be characteristic not only of all so-called behavior (those stories which are projected out into "action"), but also of all those internal stories, the sequences of the building up of the sea anemone. Its embryology must be somehow made of the stuff of stories. And behind that, again, the evolutionary process through millions of generations whereby the sea anemone, like you and like me, came to be – that process, too, must be of the stuff of stories. There must be relevance in every step of phylogeny and among the steps.

Prospero says, "We are such stuff as dreams are made on," and surely he is nearly right. But I sometimes think that dreams are only fragments of that stuff. It is as if the stuff of which we are made were totally transparent and therefore imperceptible and as if the only appearances of which we can be aware are cracks and planes of fracture in that transparent matrix. Dreams and precepts and stories are perhaps cracks and irregularities in the uniform and timeless matrix

Mind and Nature 13–14

Bateson claim that the world is made of the stuff of stories, provides another context for this important statement made by Ballard about his poetics:

It seems to me that the function of the writer is no longer the addition of fiction in the world, but rather to seek its abstraction, to direct an enquiry aimed at recovering elements of reality from this debauch of fiction

EM 76[6]

As we have seen, Bateson, in *Mind and Nature*, quotes Prospero's claim that "We are such stuff/As dreams are made on, and our little life/Is rounded with a sleep" (Shakespeare 181), in order to suggest that in the fractures of the rational world, of which dreams are an example, we are able to glimpse beyond the maps constructed by our mind at the territory itself. At one point Ballard uses Caliban, another character from *The Tempest*, to present an extreme view of the human race,

---

6 A similar statement occurs in the Preface to *Crash*: "We live inside an enormous novel. For the writer in particular it is less and less necessary for him to invent the fictional content of his novel. The fiction is already there. The writer's task is to invent the reality" (C 9).

The Atrocity Exhibition. Entering the exhibition, Travis sees the atrocities of Vietnam and the Congo mimetized in the 'alternate' death of Elizabeth Taylor; he tends the dying film star, eroticizing her punctured bronchus in the over-ventilated verandas of the London Hilton; he dreams of Max Ernst, superior of the birds; 'Europe after the Rain'; *the human race – Caliban asleep across a mirror smeared with vomit* [emphasis mine].

AE 12

However the connection between Caliban and a mirror does not originate in the Shakespearian text itself for there the subhuman son of Sycorax does not have a mirror. It comes instead from Oscar Wilde's preface to his novel *The Picture of Dorian Gray*, published in 1891, where he wrote, "the nineteenth century dislike of Realism is the rage of Caliban seeing his own face in a glass. The nineteenth century dislike of Romanticism is the rage of Caliban not seeing his own face in a glass" (3). For Wilde, the reactionary bourgeoisie of his time are like Caliban, resistant to any civilizing influence: when the art of realism accurately imitates them, they are insulted in seeing themselves represented in a such an unflattering way, but when the romantic art offers an alternative, they protest because they do not see anything that looks like them.

This motif recurs in the first chapter of James Joyce's *Ulysses* (1922), in which Stephen Dedalus is looking at himself in the mirror offered to him by Buck Mulligan, commenting "[...] The rage of Caliban at not seeing his face in a mirror. If Wilde were only alive to see you!" Dedalus answers: "[...] It is a symbol of Irish art. The cracked looking-glass of a servant" (6). Stephen claims that the way the Irish people see themselves is through a cracked mirror.

A third example can be found in Auden's 1944 poem *The Sea and the Mirror*, a dramatic commentary on *The Tempest*, which contains a long prose chapter entitled "Caliban to the Audience." The mirror of Auden's title is a symbol of art, while the sea is a symbol of life. The critic and poet John Fuller says that, in Auden's poem, Prospero may represent the artist, Ariel his imagination and Caliban his physical and corporal nature that cannot be assimilated in the world that Prospero and Ariel (namely the artist with his imagination) have created. But in the end Caliban and Ariel, body and spirit, will be precariously but lovingly united (Fuller 367–368).

In using the mirror of Caliban as a metaphor, Ballard thus draws on a rich and complex accumulation of poetic associations in which he too offers a metaphor for art and for his poetics: "The human race – Caliban asleep across a mirror smeared with vomit" (*AE* 12). For Bateson, the fundamental evolutionary unit is the organism plus its surroundings and in *The Atrocity Exhibition* we see the body exteriorized in the surrounding environment as it is perceived by the characters. Furthermore, this evolutionary unit has the same traits as the mind: a *creatural* world governed by a mental determinism. If, in the rational world at the service of binary logic the territory is not describable, then it may be through the language of dreams that Korzybski's territory, the thing-in-itself, is at least perceivable. In this sense the dream world of Caliban and the minds of the insane characters of *The Atrocity Exhibition* share the possibility of a revelation of the territory behind the map. Ballard's powerful image of Caliban, rich with surrealist undertones, encapsulates what has been said so far: the mirror is a symbol of art and it is smeared with the rejections – the atrocities – of the drunken and asleep monster, for Ballard a symbol for the human race. But this mirror can also attempt to reflect the "fractures" of the rational world, trying to show the territory rather than the map constructed by the mind. The condensed novels that compose the text are pictures or paintings of "transformational grammars" (*AE* 62) that try to disclose "the pattern which connects" (Bateson *Mind and Nature* 8). They are kernel narratives of a sort that transmit new information, thus changing a deeply-rooted *pleromatic* conception of existence to a *creatural* view of the world.

Works Cited

Auden, W.H. *The Sea and the Mirror: A Commentary on Shakespeare's* The Tempest in *Collected Poems*. New York: Vintage Books, 1991. 401–445.

Bateson, Gregory. *Mind and Nature: A Necessary Unit*. New York: E.P. Dutton, 1979.

Bateson, Gregory. *Steps to an Ecology of Mind: Collected Essays in Anthropology, Psychiatry, Evolution and Epistemology*. [1972]. London: Jason Aronson Inc., 1987.

Baxter, Jeannette. Ed. *J.G. Ballard: Contemporary Critical Perspectives*. London: Continuum, 2008.

Baxter, Jeannette. *J.G. Ballard's Surrealist Imagination: Spectacular Authorship*. Farnham: Ashgate, 2009.

Blackburn, Simon. *Oxford Dictionary of Philosophy*, Oxford: Oxford University Press, 2005.

Brier, Søren. "Cybernetics." In *The Routledge Companion to Literature and Science*. Edited by Bruce Clarke and Manuela Rossini. London: Routledge, 2011. 89–99.

Fuller, John. "The Sea and the Mirror." In *W.H. Auden: A Commentary*. London: Faber and Faber, 2007. 356–368.

Greenland, Colin. *The Entropy Exhibition: Michael Moorcock and the British "New Wave" in Science Fiction*. London: Routledge, 1983.

Günter Holl, Hans. "Second thoughts on Gregory Bateson and Alfred Korzybski" in *Kybernetes* 36: 7/8 (2007): 1047–1054.

Joyce, James. *Ulysses: Annotated Student Edition.* [1922]. London: Penguin, 2011.

Korzybski, Alfred. "A Non-Aristotelian System and Its Necessity For Rigour in Mathematics and Physics" in *Science and Sanity: An Introduction to Non-Aristotelian Systems and General Semantics.* [1933]. New York: Institute of General Semantics, 2000. 747–761.

Luckhurst, Roger. *"The Angle Between Two Walls": The Fiction of J.G. Ballard.* Liverpool: Liverpool University Press, 1997.

Morgan, Ted. *Literary Outlaw: The Life and Times of William S. Burroughs.* London: The Bodley Head, 1991.

Mosse, George L. *Toward the Final Solution: A History of European Racism.* London: J.M. Dent & Sons Ltd., 1978.

O'Hara, Dan. "Reading Posture and Gesture in Ballard's Novels" in *J.G. Ballard: Visions and Revisions.* Edited by Jeannette Baxter, Rowland Wymer. New York: Palgrave Macmillan, 2012. 105–120.

Pula, Robert P. "Alfred Korzybski, 1879–1950: A Bio-Methodological Sketch" in *Polish American Studies* 53: 2 (Autumn 1996): 57–105.

Sellars, Simon. "'Extreme Possibilities': Mapping 'the sea of time and space' in J.G. Ballard's Pacific Fictions." *Colloquy* 17 (August 2009): 44–61.

Shakespeare, William. *The Tempest.* [1611]. Oxford: Oxford University Press, 1994.

Wilde, Oscar. *The Picture of Dorian Gray.* [1890] Oxford: Oxford University Press, 2008.

CHAPTER 7

"The Logic of the Visible at the Service of the Invisible": Reading Invisible Literature in *The Atrocity Exhibition*

Elizabeth Stainforth

Abstract

Inner space and the exploration of alternative psychic realities are important themes in the fiction of J.G. Ballard. In his 1966 essay, "The Coming of the Unconscious," Ballard identifies the Surrealist origins of inner space, suggesting that the art movement was the first to make apparent "the logic of the visible at the service of the invisible." Ballard's adoption of literary collage, which features most prominently in the 1970 novel *The Atrocity Exhibition*, also indicates the influence of Surrealism on a formal level. An extension of this influence can be found in the concept of invisible literature, Ballard's term for a type of marginal reading material. These texts, examples of which include scientific reports, company brochures and advertising leaflets, aided his use of the collage technique, as well as reflecting the idea of alternative fictional realities. Furthermore, they raise questions about the extent to which meaning, for Ballard, was in the margins of reality, even beyond the inner space of his novels. This chapter addresses the significance of invisible literature, and is divided into a discussion of Ballard's reading and collecting habits, and a comparative analysis of *The Atrocity Exhibition* with specific "invisible" texts.

Keywords

J.G. Ballard – *The Atrocity Exhibition* – invisible literature – inner space – borderzone – collage – Surrealism – *Ambit* – Eduardo Paolozzi

⸻

The borderzone, the idea of a space between, is an important theme in the novels of J.G. Ballard, from the liminal sites of car parks and underpasses in *Crash* (1973) and *Concrete Island* (1974), to the neural intervals and angles between walls that pervade his experimental fiction, notably *The Atrocity Exhibition* (1970). As Roger Luckhurst observes, "Ballard, it might be said, is in the place of the hinge, the device which at once joins together and separates two planes or surfaces" (xiii). The position of the hinge is also reflected in the Ballardian trope of "inner space," a "fusion of the outer world of reality and the inner world of the psyche" (*R/S JGB* 102) that underpins the imaginative landscapes of his stories and the interior obsessions of his characters. This imaginative frame for reality is Surrealist in origin (Baxter, *Spectacular Authorship* 6). In "The Coming of the Unconscious," Ballard writes that "the images of surrealism are the iconography of inner space," identifying the art movement as the first to make apparent "the logic of the visible at the service of the invisible" (*R/S JGB* 102) in a quote borrowed from the painter Odilon Redon. Redon's phrase peculiarly echoes a concept that represents another manifestation of the borderzone in Ballard, the textual borderzone of invisible literature. His self-conscious coining of this term implies a clear rationale for a type of reading matter, which is "part of that universe of published material to which most literate people never have access" (*UGM* 182). A list of the kinds of things included in the scope of invisible literature was given in a 1970 interview in *Books and Bookmen*, when he stated:

> I have always been a voracious reader of what I term "invisible literature" – market research reports, pharmaceutical company house magazines, the promotional copy for a new high-energy breakfast food, Journals such as *Psychological Abstracts* and the Italian automobile magazine *Style Auto*, the internal memoranda of TV company planning departments, sex manuals, U.S. government reports, and medical textbooks such as the extraordinary *Crash Injuries* [...]
>
> *R/S JGB* 156

Here, it is possible to gain a sense of the marginal texts that occupy spaces beyond orthodox reading practices, at once specialist in their subject focus but ephemeral and instrumental in their purpose: what in other terms might be called the grey literature of contemporary society. Furthermore, they register a literary space between Ballard's novels, which constitutes both a conceptual and stylistic influence. His admission that short stories such as "Princess Margaret's Facelift" were taken from a medical textbook's description of a plastic surgery operation testifies to the relevance of these texts (*AE* 180), as well as gesturing towards the collage techniques of the Surrealists who inspired him. The heavy use of scientific and technical terminology and the language of the mass media are likewise features of Ballard's writing that have been widely commented on by critics.[1] However, less sustained critical attention has been

---

1   See, for example, Jeannette Baxter, *J.G. Ballard's Surrealist Imagination: Spectacular Authorship* (59–98), Roger Luckhurst, *"The Angle Between Two Walls": The Fiction of J G. Ballard* and Andrzej Gasiorek, *J.G. Ballard.*

given to the study of invisible literature[2] and the idea of Ballard as a distinctive sort of reader in relation to his writing.

In this chapter, I will address the significance of such texts, in terms of their supplementary value to Ballard's literary archive and with regard to their reappearance at a narrative and formal level in his novels. The discussion is therefore divided into two sections; the first will provide the background to Ballard's interest in invisible literature, from the early part of his writing career working at the offices of a scientific journal, through to the material he collected by way of his friendships and collaborations with other writers, artists and scientists. A survey of Ballard's collecting habits raises the question of reconstructing his invisible library as an object of study, which has been the point of departure for an online project. The second section will be framed by the perspective of the writer as reader, with reference to Jeannette Baxter's work on the uncanny effects of reading Ballard's non-fiction. Her claim that these effects are "born precisely out of the inability to identify, and therefore efface, the difference between fact and fiction" ("Uncanny Fictions" 59) is the basis for my analysis of invisible literature in *The Atrocity Exhibition*.

Collecting Invisible Literature

The idea of invisible literature first took on a recognizable form while Ballard was working for the journal *Chemistry & Industry*, where he was the deputy editor and a writer from 1958 to 1964. Of his time there he later recalled, "the office of any scientific magazine is the most wonderful mail drop. It's the ultimate information crossroads [...] I was filtering all this extraordinary material" ("Shanghai Jim"). This was the period during which he produced "Project for a New Novel," a series of photocopied collages that are described as the "sample pages of a new kind of novel, entirely consisting of magazine-style headlines and layouts, with a deliberately meaningless text, the idea being that the imaginative content could be carried by the headlines and overall design" (*R/S JGB* 38). These were created using the graphics and fonts from texts that Ballard was encountering at work. Some were excerpts from *Chemistry & Industry* itself, as Mike Bonsall has shown ("J.G. Ballard's Experiment in Chemical Living"); others were filtered from the vast mail drop of invisible literature, a chance element that would support the use of "deliberately meaningless text."

---

2 However, commentators, notably David Pringle, have studied specific examples of this ephemera. See also Mike Holliday, "Three Levels of Reality: J.G. Ballard's 'Court Circular,'" Rick McGrath, "J.G. Ballard's Graphic Experiments" and Mike Bonsall, "J.G. Ballard's Experiment in Chemical Living."

Ballard's involvement in the quarterly art and literature journal, *Ambit*, further enabled and fed his appetite for invisible literature. The paediatrician and novelist Dr Martin Bax founded *Ambit* in 1959 and Ballard became the prose editor in the mid-1960s. He soon enlisted the artist and sculptor Eduardo Paolozzi to the editorial team, having been an admirer of his work for some time. A visit to the exhibition "This is Tomorrow" at London's Whitechapel Gallery in 1956, which featured the group piece *Patio and Pavilion*, first introduced Ballard to Paolozzi's work. To Ballard's eye, the combination of found objects resembled the remnants of civilization after a nuclear disaster (*ML* 187–188). During this period, Paolozzi also made a number of text-image works, some versions of which would later appear in *Ambit*.[3]

Paolozzi's fusion of image-making and literature complemented Ballard's visual prose style and both were interested in Surrealism. Adopting Surrealist collage techniques, *Ambit* became a testing ground for their experimental ideas, which typically combined literary prose with mass media images and technical language. Ballard and Paolozzi sometimes collaborated, producing several graphic projects which combined text and media images. The first of these, "Moonstrips" and "General Dynamic F.U.N.," appeared in *Ambit* No. 33 in 1967 and was adapted from Paolozzi's print series, *Moonstrips Empire News* (1967), interspersing familiar commercial icons with found phrases, amid formatting flourishes from Bax and Ballard. Later projects included *The Vietnam Symphony* with Bax (*Ambit* No. 63, 1975) and *Images for J.G.B* (*Ambit* No. 83, 1980). Re-using and recontextualizing previous works was part of a conscious practice for Paolozzi, through which the relationships between his artworks were reconfigured. Of these processes, David Brittain writes:

> He [Paolozzi] embraced notions of recycling and transformation as metaphors for the creative process. By re-use and repetition, the artist suggests sub-texts, narratives and continuities within and between his various art works. (12–13)

The notion of recycling highlights another parallel with Ballard, since he adopted a comparable method in "Project for a New Novel," and for a fake advertising campaign, published in *Ambit* between 1967 and 1970. In the former, the names Coma and Kline emerge, then reappearing as characters in *The Atrocity Exhibition*. The adverts include themes of inner space and lists of figures and places (Ralph Nader, Dealey Plaza, Zapruder) that would similarly recur time and again. The material for these projects was partly provided through Ballard's association with Paolozzi, who made many of his own collages from the huge

---

3   See, for example, the print series Metafisikal Translations, produced in 1962.

image bank he accumulated throughout his lifetime. Both Ballard and Bax had access to these images and in a 1983 interview, Bax remarked:

> Eduardo has a huge image archive of material – which I think fascinated Jim very much. I suppose what Jim was interested in was Eduardo's style of collecting images of the 20th century, which struck him as something a writer should do.
>
> R/S JGB 39

Paolozzi, then, was an influential figure, his image collection and artistic practice informing Ballard's development of the collage technique. Interview comments also suggest that he and Paolozzi may have swapped sources; certainly the oft-cited *Crash Injuries* by Jacob Kulowski[4] was a shared reference, which Ballard once claimed was in a research library they were compiling together (R/S JGB 156).[5]

Of those texts that Ballard collected and shared with Paolozzi, the largest portion was likely to have come from the scientist Dr Christopher Evans, a close friend of Ballard's, who supplied him with a wealth of scientific papers and advertising brochures from the circulars that were sent to his office every week. Talking to Thomas Frick in *The Paris Review*, Ballard explained:

> For years, Dr Christopher Evans, a psychologist in the computer branch of the National Physical Laboratory literally sent me the contents of his wastebasket. Once a fortnight, a huge envelope arrived filled with scientific reprints and handouts, specialist magazines and reports, all of which I read carefully.
>
> "THE ART OF FICTION"

All the ephemera he amassed were kept in his coal-shed, which he would describe, aptly, as "the most potent compost for the imagination" (UGM 182). Indeed, it could be argued that the literary counterpart to Paolozzi's image archive is Ballard's library of invisible literature. Yet, whereas the bulk of Paolozzi's papers are now held in the National Galleries of Scotland's archive, Ballard eventually cleared out his coal-shed, admitting in a 1990 interview,

---

4   See also Sam Francis, "'Moral Pornography' and 'Total Imagination': The Pornographic in J.G. Ballard's *Crash*," Mark Dery, "An Extremely Complicated Phenomenon of a Very Brief Duration Ending in Destruction: The 20th Century as Slow-motion Car Crash," Nicolas Daly, *Literature, Technology, and Modernity, 1860–2000* and Dennis A. Foster, *Sublime Enjoyment: On the Perverse Motive in American Literature*.

5   There is no known record of the existence of this library.

"I finally cleaned it out, about five years ago, I could hardly bear to throw any of it away" ("Tales From the Dark Side"). Therefore, while he appeared to have an attachment to these items, he was ultimately willing enough to relinquish them and to maintain their invisibility. This tendency, to sift and actively erase material, is discernible in other cases too. As has been noted (Hall, "Relics of a Red-hot Mind"), Ballard's official archive, held in the British Library, is conspicuous in its orderliness. Chris Beckett, who catalogued the archive, cautions that:

> Their contents will disappoint the customs officials of biographical research [...] The sparkle and clutter of everyday ephemera that will often swell collections of personal papers in enlightening ways is entirely absent from Ballard's archive. (3)

The absence was obviously intended by Ballard, who expressed his distaste for the practice of archiving, whereby redundant papers are accorded the status of valuable documents (*R/S JGB* 34); with regard to his published work, only manuscript drafts and the associated notes survive.

However, considering his evident fascination with invisible literature, the idea of uncovering Ballard's lost library, of making the invisible visible, remains a tantalizing prospect for researchers. Of course, on one level it is an impossible task. Many of the original papers were destroyed and, while Paolozzi's archive might offer insights into material Ballard was collecting during his time at *Ambit*, it could not shed light on those texts he gathered and stored himself. On the other hand, Ballard made several specific references to the invisible literature that inspired his stories (e.g. *AE* 123 and *R/S JGB* 10; 20), a starting point for compiling a list. In addition, it is now easier to locate previously unavailable sources through Internet searches and bibliographic e-databases, as well as information sharing in online forums.[6] This kind of thinking provides the background for the web-based project "The Invisible Library,"[7] which is a collaborative, open source catalogue, collected from various sources, to record the reading material Ballard came into contact with. Supported by Mike Bonsall's *Digital Ballard* website, it is possible to add entries by filling in an online web form. At the time of writing, over 600 items were recorded in the list, a combination of literary works, largely collected by David Pringle, along with more marginal texts, including obscure journals and scientific reports.

---

6 See, for example, https://groups.yahoo.com/neo/groups/jgb/info.

7 See http://fentonville.co.uk/invisible-library/. "The Invisible Library" is a collaborative project, initiated by the author and Mike Bonsall.

The mixture of what could be called visible and invisible literature in the online catalogue is reflective of Ballard's own idiosyncratic reading habits. In a list of his favourite books, originally published in Antonia Fraser's edited volume, *The Pleasure of Reading*, a 1980s copy of the Los Angeles *Yellow Pages* was included alongside *The Rime of the Ancient Mariner* and the *Collected Short Stories of Ernest Hemingway*. Ballard's ability to codify the material he consumed and develop it into an imaginative framework, through a process of reading widely and voraciously, was crucial in shaping the powerful visions evoked in his experimental writing. The most complete expression of these ideas can be found in *The Atrocity Exhibition*, some themes from which are directly attributable to invisible literature.

The Influence of Invisible Literature

The non-linear structure and fragmentary composition of *The Atrocity Exhibition* makes it one of Ballard's most difficult and challenging works. Organized into 15 short stories, or "condensed novels" (*EM* 16), the narrative is mediated through the psychotic consciousness of the protagonist, named Traven, Talbert, Tallis, along with several other variations. Although it is not a collage novel in the strict sense, the style broadly corresponds with the collage aesthetic as defined by André Breton. In his view the innovatory features of collage are not to be found so much in the words or images used as in their combination; and the value of the encounter between disparate realities lies primarily in its effect (Adamowicz 4). In *The Atrocity Exhibition*, such effects take on a new dimension against the backdrop of 1960s culture. As he struggles to come to terms with his environment, the character obsessively re-enacts some of the iconic tragedies of the twentieth century, events which are notable for the unprecedented level of media coverage they received. For example, John F. Kennedy's assassination is played out again in the episode entitled "The Assassination Weapon":

> Captain Webster studied the documents laid out on Nathan's demonstration table. These were: (1) a spectroheliogram of the sun; (2) tarmac and takeoff checks for the B-29 Superfortress Enola Gay; (3) electroencephalogram of Albert Einstein; (4) transverse section through a pre-Cambrian trilobite; (5) photograph taken at noon, August 7th, 1945, of the sand-sea, Qattara Depression; (6) Max Ernst's "Garden Airplane Traps." He turned to Doctor Nathan. "You say these constitute an assassination weapon?"
>
> *AE* 46–47

Kennedy's assassination is a recurring theme, representative of a severe crisis throughout the novel. Here, Ballard effectively deploys the collage style to force a synthesis between apparently unrelated entities, reflecting the disjointed experience of the story's mental patient, who "wants to kill Kennedy again, but in a way that makes sense" (*AE 50*).

The central plot around which each episode revolves is the search for a modulus, an attempt by the character to recover some semblance of reality. Samuel Francis has suggested that this quest is "a search for the point of junction or intersection between the different levels of reality, for a point of fixity, for absolute reality itself" (89). In the passage entitled "Planes Intersect," the logic of the modulus is further elaborated:

> Planes intersect: on one level, the tragedies of Cape Kennedy and Vietnam serialized on billboards, random deaths mimetized in the experimental auto disasters of Nader and his co-workers. Their precise role in the unconscious merits closer scrutiny, by the way, they may in fact play very different parts from the ones we assign them. On another level, the immediate personal environment, the volumes of space enclosed by your opposed hands, the geometry of your postures, the time values contained in this office, the angles between these walls. On a third level, the inner world of the psyche. Where these planes intersect, images are born, some kind of valid reality begins to assert itself.
>
> *AE 72*

The extract, described by Ballard as "a methodology for discovering contemporary reality" (Francis 69), identifies reality as intersecting on three planes: the media environment, the immediate environment and the psychic environment. Preserving the psychic impulse in Surrealist collage by acknowledging the significance of the inner world, it also pinpoints the birth of the image as a clarifying event, born at the point where the three planes intersect. The coalescence of these elements implies a recovery of meaning and stems from the recognition that a contemporary understanding of the real is comprised of different levels of experience. For, as the episodes reveal, there is no one formula for locating a modulus; the geometry of buildings, the angles of apartments, the planes of a woman's face, even the dream of amniotic return are all figured as aspects of reality. This sense of fragmentation is mirrored in the portrayal of the character throughout the novel. Towards the end, we are confronted with another form of it, as he disappears from the closing sections and his story becomes embedded in the headings. As Luckhurst puts it, "(he) himself is eventually dispersed into traces, footnotes of a main document that has now been lost" (117).

Such devices are symptomatic of a more general tendency in Ballard's writing, to construct open-ended narratives, which call for a degree of interpretation. In a 1983 interview with Graeme Revell, he explained, "the character of my fiction requires the reader himself to make a significant contribution. I'm offering a kit with which the reader (can use) [...] my books as a sort of instructional manual" (*R/S JGB* 45). An extreme version of this instructional format can be found in the 1977 short story, "The Index" (*CSS2* 434–441), which consists entirely of index headings to provide clues to the plot of the missing main text, the autobiography of one Henry Rhodes Hamilton. An assemblage of dates, events and encounters with notable figures is the means by which the reader must piece it together, a contingent process that sets off a peculiarly cyclical pattern of reading and re-reading. The many lists that pervade *The Atrocity Exhibition*, produced via free association exercises (*AE* 89), work in a similar way, punctuating and disrupting the narrative. Ballard's ability to create meaningful absences and silences returns us to the question of the invisible and invisible literature. Such texts are continually hovering in and around the novel; both invented, as in Koester's journal of car accidents, *Crash!* (*AE* 28), and Bernouli's *Encyclopedia of Imaginary Diseases* (*AE* 117) and real, like the Wellcome Museum's catalogue of tropical diseases (*AE* 116). *Newsweek, Paris Match, Oggi, Vogue* and *Harpers' Bazaar* also feature in the stories, cultural references that litter the psychologized environment. In the marginal notes that first appeared in the 1990 RE/Search edition, Ballard calls the Warren Commission Report "a remarkable document" (*AE* 40) and pays tribute to the scientific report, "Tolerances of the Human Face to Crash Impact," for the title of one story that also appears on a list in the passage, "A New Algebra" (*AE* 109). In fact, the traces of collecting and studying these materials are effectively on show, implying a different, more readerly perspective, beyond the writerly device of meaningful absence, through which the texts function as cultural ciphers.

Baxter similarly highlights the readerly viewpoint in her essay on Ballard's non-fiction, which discusses the instability of textual boundaries in his writing, particularly those between fact and fiction. Therefore, as she argues, the non-fiction space represents an interesting field of study, providing an alternative mode of storytelling for Ballard ("Uncanny Fictions" 52). Repetition, revision, and re-evaluation of texts emerge as key motifs in her comparison of his reviews and commentaries and Sigmund Freud's theory of the uncanny is used to elaborate the unsettling effect of *déjà vu* ("Uncanny Fictions" 54) when reading them side by side. A parallel claim could be made for the effect of reading *The Atrocity Exhibition* alongside the invisible literature that informed it (*R/S JGB* 10), a complex dialogue between imagination and data, which, according to Ballard, reveals a form of incidental truth (*R/S JGB* 20). Of the interplay between scientific material and fiction, he stressed:

I think if you intend to do anything really original you've got to go beyond it – one's own imagination has got to come into play on some level, to begin to reshape and remake the material. It's very difficult, actually, using scientific material [...] in prose, producing fiction [...] Very few texts stand up, particularly on their own.

R/S JGB 19

The textual support necessary to transform the fiction of science into the fiction of a novel is a complex process, then, and invites closer examination of specific cases.

The 1965 report "Tolerances of the Human Face to Crash Impact" and the textbook *Crash Injuries* are among the clearest examples of the integration of invisible literature in *The Atrocity Exhibition*. The former was discovered by Ballard's girlfriend; in an introductory note to the story he writes of her realization that "here was a title waiting for its rendezvous with a Ballard fiction" (*AE* 123). But the influence of the report evidently goes beyond the imaginatively fertile title, as shown in the following:

> To obtain impact tolerance data of living human heads, auto salvage yards were searched to locate dash panels that had dents made by the right front seat passenger as he jacknifed forward during a front-end collision. These dash panels were purchased from the salvage yard and brought to the laboratory for study [...] Next, entire cowlings from identical cars (make, model and year) were purchased and impacted with an instrumented dummy head on a small catapult, until the dent made by the human head was duplicated as to area, depth and exact location on the dash.
>
> SWEARINGEN 1

The outline of a method for obtaining data about the tolerance of human heads is itself a morbidly absurd theme, reminiscent of Jacopetti's barely plausible, half-faked *Mondo Cane* documentaries (*AE* 124). It is possible to see what Ballard describes as the reshaping of such texts in the next passage, from "Crash!":

> Panels consisting of drive-in theatre personnel, students and middle-income housewives were encouraged to devise the optimum auto disaster. A wide choice of impact modes was available, including roll-over, roll-over followed by head-on collision, multiple pile-ups and motorcade attacks.
>
> AE 155

The third-person commentary and detached tone are features of both extracts and the attention to detail, measurements and control factors also carry the mark of the scientific experiment. However, in the second case the implicit violence and aggression of such testing procedures are made manifest, the incidental "impact tolerance data" replaced by the deliberate aggression of the "optimum auto disaster." It is a subtle but significant sleight of hand that subverts the objective style, in a shift from factual reportage to conceptualized desire. The narrative mode of *Crash Injuries* provokes a similar sleight of hand. The high car crash rate of 1952 gives rise to Kulowski's curiously Ballardian observation that, "the highway was then virtually turned into a laboratory for 'unscheduled' crash experiments relative to the collection and analysis of data from the epidemiological standpoint" (101). Likewise, in his survey of crash injuries, he notes specific fractures named for their association with the car:

> Most noteworthy was the 'chauffeur's fracture' of the radius which was caused by the hand crank in the starting engine. Noteworthy also was its elimination by the introduction of the self-starter. The 'bumper fracture' of the tibia and fibula has not shared a similar fate. Nor has McLanahan's [...] 'spear-like forward pointing door handle design' ceased entirely to threaten pedestrians with impalement. (93)

The earnestness of these reflections renders them darkly comical, another effect that is amplified in Ballard's re-workings:

> Involuntary orgasms during the cleaning of automobiles [...] Consultations with manufacturers have led to modifications of rear trim and styling, in order to neutralize these erogenous zones, or if possible transfer them to more socially acceptable areas within the passenger compartment.
>
> *AE* 142

Throughout *The Atrocity Exhibition*, the references to roll-over and head-on collision crashes are repeated several times; the example above comes later in the novel, while in "The University of Death" story Dr Nathan explains, "one must bear in mind that roll-over followed by a head-on collision produces complex occupant movements and injuries from unknown sources" (*AE* 30), and then in "Tolerances of the Human Face," Travers says "the impact point was here – roll-over followed by head-on collision" (*AE* 108). The obsessive re-iteration of these crash trajectories can be mapped back onto the "Planes Intersect" passage, examined earlier, the impact point signifying the real, which is also mediated via the fictional sites of the experiment, medical testimony and the media. As Karen Novotny quips before her visit to the impact zone, "we're all in the movies" (*AE* 108), a filmic take on Ballard's comment that "I treat the reality I inhabit as if it were a fiction [...] These days we're living inside an enormous novel" (*R/S JGB* 43). *The Atrocity Exhibition*'s subversion of factual sites of knowledge and authority both challenges and reinforces the fragmented experience of contemporary reality that is rationalized through a range of fictions, including invisible literature. Furthermore, Ballard's use of such texts unsettles the borderzones of the fictive, re-inscribing their location in the cultural sphere.

In its examination of invisible literature, this chapter has sought to make visible an important source of inspiration for Ballard, calling attention to him as a reader of fictions of every kind (*JGB* 98–100). Only traces of these reading practices and texts are discernible, their residue creating the strange, unsettling tone of *The Atrocity Exhibition*. Throughout the discussion, the question of the borderzone has been raised several times, to suggest various conceptual relations and partitions; visible and invisible entities, inner and outer worlds, fictional and factual realities. If, as Ballard proposed, it is the intersection of different planes of experience, the border itself that allows for glimpses of contemporary reality, then perhaps a similar idea can be applied on a textual level. Without doubt, the open-ended form of Ballard's writing constitutes one element of this juncture, the presence of the invisible rendered to powerful effect in stories like "The Index." However, as demonstrated, the juxtaposition between the fictional reality of *The Atrocity Exhibition* and the factual narratives of invisible literature also spawns insights about how narrow the spaces between them can be; in Ballard, the constant negotiation of borders produces a sharp, unflinching commentary on the pathological aspects of everyday life (*AE* 128). As such, by exploring their parameters further, here I have suggested an inversion of Redon's Surrealist logic by placing the invisible at the service of the visible.

Works Cited

Adamowicz, Elza. *Surrealist Collage in Text and Image: Dissecting the Exquisite Corpse.* Cambridge: Cambridge University Press, 1998.

Ballard, J.G. "Shanghai Jim." BBC documentary, dir. James Runcie, 1990.

Ballard, J.G. and Thomas Frick. "Interviews: The Art of Fiction." *Paris Review* 94 (1984). Web. 21 July 2015.

Ballard, J.G. and Luc Sante. "Tales From the Dark Side." *The New York Times*, 9 September 1990. Web. 21 July 2015.

Baxter, Jeannette. *J.G. Ballard's Surrealist Imagination: Spectacular Authorship*. Farnham: Ashgate, 2009.

Baxter, Jeannette. "Uncanny Fictions: Reading Ballard's 'Non-Fiction.'" *J.G. Ballard: Visions and Revisions*. Edited by Jeannette Baxter and Rowland Wymer. London: Palgrave Macmillan, 2011. 50–70.

Beckett, Chris. "The Progress of the Text: The Papers of J.G. Ballard at the British Library." *Electronic British Library Journal* (2011), Article 12. Web. 21 July 2015.

Bonsall, Mike. "J.G. Ballard's Experiment in Chemical Living." *Ballardian*, 1 August 2007. Web. 21 July 2015.

Brittain, David. *The Jet Age Compendium: Paolozzi at Ambit*. London: Four Corners Books, 2009.

Daly, Nicholas. *Literature, Technology, and Modernity, 1860–2000*. Cambridge: Cambridge University Press, 2004.

Dery, Mark. "An Extremely Complicated Phenomenon of a Very Brief Duration Ending in Destruction: The 20th Century as Slow-motion Car Crash." *TechnoMorphica*, 1997.

Foster, Dennis A. *Sublime Enjoyment: On the Perverse Motive in American Literature*. Cambridge: Cambridge University Press, 1997.

Francis, Samuel. "Image in the Contemporary: *The Atrocity Exhibition*." *A Critical Reading of "Inner Space" in Selected Works of J.G. Ballard*. University of Leeds PhD Thesis.

Francis, Sam. "'Moral Pornography' and 'Total Imagination': The Pornographic in J.G. Ballard's *Crash*." *English: Journal of the English Association* 57:218 (2008): 146–168.

Fraser, Antonia. Ed. *The Pleasure of Reading*. London: Bloomsbury, 1992.

Gasiorek, Andrzej. *J.G. Ballard*. Manchester: Manchester University Press, 2005.

Hall, Chris. "J.G. Ballard: Relics of a Red-hot Mind." *The Guardian*, 4 August 2011. Web. 21 July 2015.

Holliday, Mike. "Three Levels of Reality: J.G. Ballard's 'Court Circular.'" *Ballardian*, 11 January 2009. Web. 21 July 2015.

Kulowski, Jacob. *Crash Injuries: the Integrated Medical Aspects of Automobile Injuries and Deaths*. Springfield, Ill: Charles C. Thomas, 1960.

Luckhurst, Roger. *"The Angle Between Two Walls": The Fiction of J.G. Ballard*. Liverpool: Liverpool University Press, 1997.

McGrath, Rick. "J.G. Ballard's Graphic Experiments." *Adventure Thru Inner Space: Essays and Articles*, 2008. Web. 21 July 2015.

Swearingen, John J. "Tolerances of the Human Face to Crash Impact." Federal Aviation Agency, July 1965. Web. 5 August 2015.

Warren E. "Report of the President's Commission on the Assassination of President Kennedy." Washington: United States Government Printing Office, 1964. The U.S. National Archives and Records Administration. Web. 5 August 2015.

CHAPTER 8

Hidden Heterotopias in *Crash*

Christopher Duffy

Abstract

Located in and around the motorway space, multiple sites in *Crash* resemble Marc Augé's concept of non-place. This chapter examines the way in which J.G. Ballard's appropriation of non-place endows these sites with subversive meaning and imaginative potential. The motorway location in *Crash* is disturbed by a series of hidden enclaves rebelliously established within its space. These enclaves further recall Michel Foucault's heterotopias of illusion that highlight the enclosure and partitioning of space all around them. *Crash* may be explored in terms of tensions between heterotopia and non-place operating around discourses of seeing and not seeing. Ballard's text defiantly reads the motorway as an experimental space open to different kinds of access that challenge proscriptive, official, and correct use. The personalized car cabin, marked by the presence of the owner, is an important heterotopic site hidden from the outside gaze of authority. The characters of *Crash* wilfully misuse tactics employed by authorities to regulate space, including documentary evidence such as statistical reports and photographs. Each spatial intervention by authority becomes a potential point of resistance, and the smooth running of non-place is interrupted in order to recover hidden meanings.

Keywords

J.G. Ballard – *Crash* – space – motorway – non-place – heterotopia – embodied driving – governmentality – science – technology – resistance – Michel Foucault – Marc Augé

> Really, it's not the car that's important: it's *driving*.
> J.G. BALLARD interviewed by LYNN BARBER, 1970 (*EM* 31).

This chapter examines *Crash* (1973) in terms of a dialogue between theories of heterotopia and non-place, highlighting the way in which space can be appropriated to challenge critical discourses about proper use. Ballard's novel focuses on a series of enclaves resistant to the increasing prevalence of homogenized space within the urban environment. These enclaves are locations where alternative orderings of the social can be imagined and experimented on. Recognising the increasing prevalence of non-place in contemporary society theorised by Marc Augé, *Crash* concentrates on a series of sites that resemble Michel Foucault's concept of heterotopia. I want to highlight the motorway as a central space in *Crash* open to alternative kinds of access, considering the idea of embodied driving and the hidden car cabin allowing characters to open resistive spaces within the motorway non-place. The "coming autogeddon" (C 37) of *Crash* focuses on space utilised in an imaginative way, recognizing the potential of the motorway as an experimental and subversive site defying proscriptive, official, and correct use. The fluid space of the road generates a number of anxieties about governance of space that Ballard's text actively subverts.

As Ballard recounts, the genesis or "gene" (AE 157) for *Crash* was the chapter "Crash!" in *The Atrocity Exhibition* (1970), a story that announces "The latent sexual content of the automobile crash" (AE 153). *The Atrocity Exhibition* obsesses over environments comprised of motorways and embankments, describing a conflation of internal and external spaces: "The concrete landscape of underpass and overpass mediated a more real presence, the geometry of a neural interval, the identity latent within his own musculature" (AE 20). As Ballard commented in 1970, the same year as publication of *The Atrocity Exhibition*:

> I think the twentieth century reaches just about its highest expression on the highway. Everything is there, the speed and violence of our age, its love of stylisation, fashion, the organisational side of things – what I call the elaborately signalled landscape.
>
> EM 31

By recognizing the organizational side of things, contrasted with the imaginative investments of stylization and fashion, Ballard acknowledges the regulatory effects of motorway space on human behaviour. With *Crash*, Ballard takes the opportunity to carry out a sustained and focused investigation of the motorway's elaborately signalled landscape in a way precluded by the dizzying multiplicity of concerns in *The Atrocity Exhibition*. As several critics have noted, whilst *Crash* emerges out of *The Atrocity Exhibition*, its form is very different. For Roger Luckhurst, the "move from the polylogue of *The Atrocity Exhibition* to the remorseless monologism of *Crash* is a startling transition" (123), whilst Jeannette Baxter observes, "Following *The Atrocity Exhibition*'s promiscuity of forms, *Crash* stages a contest of pornographic forms – encyclopaedia (perverse taxonomies) versus collage (metaphorical obscenity) – which works to criticize and reinvigorate tired textual and sexual narratives through an imaginative exercise in obscene parody" (114). The radically different textual structure of *Crash* sacrifices the disparate and fragmentary collage effects of *The Atrocity Exhibition,* substituting the single obsessive voice of narrator James Ballard for the wildly modulating persona of the T-cell. This focus allows Ballard to isolate and investigate the motorway space that informs *The Atrocity Exhibition,* and *Crash* expands on themes of externalizing hidden spaces: the neural intervals and latent identities explored in Ballard's earlier text. The fascination with the contemporary landscape emerging out of *The Atrocity Exhibition* is elaborated on in *Crash,* and a dialogue is set up between the two texts. Certain important features are carried over, and it is possible to see informative echoes of *The Atrocity Exhibition* in the obsessional lists of car crash injuries in *Crash.* Similar inspirations can also be traced in the "invisible literature" (*R/S JGB* 156) informing both, a pertinent example being the "rendezvous" of John J. Swearingen's 1965 text, "Tolerances of the Human Face to Crash Impact" with Ballard's fiction (*C* 99, *AE* 123). Ballard's two books therefore remain intrinsically linked, with *Crash* growing from and expanding on the fertile motorway spaces of *The Atrocity Exhibition.*

For Samuel Francis, the phrase "benevolent psychopathology" (*C* 112) is central to his late-Freudian reading of *Crash,* and Ballard's text "is precisely concerned with the new psychological possibilities of the machine landscape [...] which might enable human beings to reconnect with the alienating surfaces of their high-tech environment" (108). Such psychological possibilities are resistive to officially sanctioned uses of the machine landscape, accessing space in an unofficial and imaginative way. *Crash* investigates the motorway as a component of the contemporary environment that, in affluent western society, touches the lives of everybody. Andrzej Gasiorek notes the brilliance of *Crash* "derives in part from its overdetermined nature: it can never finally decide what kind of text it is – a moral tract, or paean to the joys of sexual violence? This indecision makes it a liminal work that blurs the boundary between the moral and the immoral, and it keeps crossing back and forth between these discourses" (18). The spatiality of *Crash* problematizes normative moral judgements, opening a series of enclaves that operate in spaces suspended between correct and incorrect behaviour. For Baxter, *Crash* is a work of "serious protest" with the violence of the text opening up disavowed histories: "the official, instantaneous reaction to this violent display of contorted flesh and metal is to whitewash its history. With cautious brushstrokes the underlying physical and psychological realities of the car crash are overlaid and concealed before being swept aside out of view. It is precisely this repression of material realities by dominant cultural systems which Ballard's art counters" (103). The recovery of a car crash swept aside by officials can also be considered in spatial terms, as a rebellious enclave opened up in the officiated space of the motorway.

Two important contexts for my reading of space in *Crash* are Foucault's idea of heterotopia and Augé's concept of non-place. Augé has called the conglomeration of contemporary transport and transit spaces non-places:

> If a place can be defined as relational, historical and concerned with identity, then a space which cannot be defined as relational, or historical, or concerned with identity will be a non-place. The hypothesis advanced here is that supermodernity produces non-places, meaning spaces which are not themselves anthropological places and which [...] do not integrate with earlier places. (63)

Non-places resist easy interpretation by denying the validity of their own history as in itself meaningful, becoming self-enclosed and self-referential only to other non-places. They are spaces produced by the current epoch which Augé calls supermodernity. For Augé, non-places necessitate a certain understanding of space, and "the word 'non-place' designates two complementary but distinct realities: spaces formed in relation to certain ends (transport, transit, commerce, leisure), and the relations that individuals have with these spaces" (76). The concept investigates both the logic of supermodernity as prioritising the movement of people, goods, and commerce, and the way in which the individual is integrated within space. This underlying organizational logic means that non-places are predicated on the slackening of communal ties so that people can be moved without resistance: "As anthropological places create the organically social, so non-places create solitary contractuality" (76). The individual is a target within non-place because they are spaces reliant on the movement of free and unburdened commercial agents. In contrast to places shaped and orientated to the use of local inhabitants, non-places are designed as transitory and mobile, promoting the free flow of movement. Non-places are spaces occupied by shoppers, commuters, migrants, or transitory workers. The increasingly prevalence of non-places means that occupied space becomes less about the needs of a small community of individuals, and is instead abstracted by the demands of a global flow of capital.

Luckhurst notes that *Crash* takes place in and around a series of non-places. The motorway is the most prominent example, but airports and hospitals are also important. For Luckhurst, the non-places described in *Crash* are unstable and unable to fully displace or erase "recalcitrant traces" (131) of the past, which return in a process of uncanny haunting. *Crash* can be read as a text which systematically destabilizes non-place, but emphasis should also be placed on the agency of characters in the text to bring about their own alternative readings of space enabling acts of resistance.

In contrast to non-place, Foucault's concept of heterotopia, which literally means "other spaces," describes alternative spaces to the normal or everyday. The concept helps define the unruly alternative spaces opened up in *Crash*. Heterotopias are:

> real places, effective places, places that are written into the institution of society itself, and that are a sort of counter-emplacements, a sort of effectively realized utopias in which the real emplacements, all the other real emplacements that can be found within culture, are simultaneously represented, contested and inverted. (17)

Kevin Hetherington, using the idea of badlands, describes heterotopias as "spaces of alternative ordering. Heterotopia organize a bit of the social world in a way different to that which surrounds them" (viii). Edward W. Soja believes, "Foucault's heterogeneous and relational space of heterotopias is neither a substanceless void to be filled by cognitive intuition nor a repository of physical forms to be phenomenologically described in all its resplendent variability. It is another space [...] actually lived and socially created spatiality, concrete and abstract at the same time, the habitus of social practices" (17–18). Heterotopias are therefore actually lived spaces, socially realized but also subject to imaginative investment.

Elaborating his concept, Foucault differentiates between heterotopias of illusion and compensation. Foucault describes the role of heterotopias of illusion "to create a space of illusion that exposes all real space, all the emplacements in the interior of which human life is enclosed and partitioned, as even more illusory" (21), contrasted with heterotopias of compensation that express the desire to create space "that is as ordered and meticulous as the remainder is disordered, messy and mixed up" (Boyer 54). Heterotopias of compensation bring to mind Foucault's work on ordered pieces of space directed towards the creation of docile bodies. The relationship between heterotopias of compensation and illusion is antagonistic in that it is precisely the excessive and arbitrary ordering of space that heterotopias of illusion expose. Heterotopias of illusion are therefore potentially resistive spaces, and a possibility held open is that heterotopias of compensation could be exposed by accessing them in imaginative and rebellious ways. In one example pertinent to the themes of *Crash*, Foucault describes an American motel room "where one goes with one's car and one's mistress and where illicit sex is both absolutely sheltered and absolutely hidden, kept isolated without, however, being left in the open" (21). The motel is a regulated space open to public access, but within this space the inhabitants are able to kept illicit sex hidden from view.

Baxter notes that the narrative of James Ballard in *Crash* is "replete with verbs pertaining to multiple ways of seeing – to spectate, to witness, to see, to visualise, to watch, to look and to observe" (101). The different ways of seeing in *Crash* correlates with an equally important discourse of not seeing. The operation of the non-place of the motorway relies on users not seeing Luckhurst's recalcitrant traces that Ballard's text attempts to bring to the open. Similarly, the tension between Foucault's heterotopias of illusion and compensation is arranged around discourses of seeing and not seeing. Ordered and meticulous, heterotopias of compensation attempt to make their space visible, as opposed to absolutely hidden heterotopias of illusion such as Foucault's motel room. A heterotopic reading of *Crash* reveals it as a text suffused with hidden spaces established within the seemingly open and visible space of the motorway. The text also subverts a series of visualizing technologies, such as documentary and scientific evidence, that attempt to bring the event of the car crash into a transparent realm of knowledge.

The motorway space explored in *Crash* is identified by Augé as a prime example of non-place:

> The real non-places of supermodernity – the ones we inhabit when we are driving down the motorway [...] have the peculiarity that they are defined partly by the words and texts they offer us: their 'instructions for use', which may be prescriptive ('Take right-hand lane'), prohibitive ('No smoking') or informative ('You are now entering the Beaujolais region'). Sometimes these are couched in more or less explicit and codified ideograms (on road signs, maps and tourist guides), sometimes in ordinary language. (77–78)

The motorway is a space which is cut through with prohibitions and regulatory information in the form of instructional words and texts. It is governed by a set of rules, boldly announced by road signs dictating access and use, attempting to guarantee the smooth operation of space. The motorway necessitates constant movement and slackens the possibility of any localized or communal ties within its space. Motorways are zones of transit that the user passes through without really noticing. The driver does not remain long enough to build meaningful spatial relationships. Attention is constantly shifted away from the possibilities of other kinds of surrounding space:

Main roads no longer pass through towns, but lists of their notable features – and, indeed, a whole commentary – appear on big signboards nearby. In a sense the traveller is absolved of the need to stop or even look [...] The landscape keeps its distance, but its natural or architectural details give rise to a text, sometimes supplemented by a schematic plan when it appears that the passing traveller is not really in a position to see the remarkable feature drawn to his attention, and thus has to derive what pleasure he can from the mere knowledge of its proximity.

AUGÉ 78–79

This distancing is a prominent feature of *Crash*. The motorway abstracts other spaces and landscapes, constituting knowledge through proximity rather than direct experience. As Sebastian Groes notes, Ballard's description of motorways resemble a distinctly American form of road building that accentuates automation:

The American system of motorways is characterized by fluidity and movement and reduces space to a pure Idea, which is the opposite of the stasis of the European city, with its mass organized around the unity of a social centre. There is a paradox at the heart of driving an automobile: 'auto,' etymologically derived from 'self,' suggests that it is the subject who is in control of his or her mobility, but the opposite is happening. The autonomous subject is subjected to a process, a collective experience in which (s)he is a figure whose unconscious yields control. (128)

In *Crash*, James Ballard contemplates his domestic space bounded and contained by the surrounding motorway system:

Our own apartment house at Drayton Park stood a mile to the north of the airport in a pleasant island of modern housing units, landscaped filling stations and supermarkets, shielded from the distant bulk of London by an access spur of the northern circular motorway which flowed past us on its elegant concrete pillars. I gazed down at the immense motion sculpture, whose traffic deck seemed almost higher than the balcony rail against which I leaned. I began to orientate myself again round its reassuring bulk, its familiar perspectives of speed, purpose and direction.

C 36

The speed, purpose and direction of the motorway pulls the surrounding environment into its orbit, shielding it from the intrusion of the outside space of

London. Anonymous housing units, filling stations, and supermarkets become features of a landscape dwarfed by the towering traffic deck of the motorway. James Ballard observes "the human inhabitants of this technological landscape no longer provided its sharpest pointers, its keys to the borderzones of identity" (*C* 36). The dominance of the motorway supplants direct experience of the landscape that includes James Ballard's home environment.

Augé draws attention to the motorway as a non-place that must be accessed in the correct way by keeping to the right side of the road, obeying the speed limit, and so on. These rules are announced by a familiar series of signs dictating proper use. In the UK, the question of proper use has been troubling authorities since the building of the first inter-urban motorway, the M1 between London and Leeds, in 1959. Peter Merriman's study of the M1 perceptively notes that the motorway emerges as a space of "scientific experiment, economic calculation and death" (186). Merriman shows how the space of the motorway is a focus for "all manner of programmes of government, including seemingly large-scale (state) programmes concerned with governing others at a distance" (142). Traffic flows and their economic impacts are predicted and costed so that the motorway is recast as an experimental space in which every movement is a statistic. Attempts are made to quantify and show up incorrect use, and attention is focused on "the irregular and undesirable movements and performances of both motorists *and* the motorway: the irregular movements of vehicles involved in accidents, the presence of broken-down vehicles, and movements or failures in the construction materials" (190). The motorway becomes a target for a series of regulatory governmental tactics since, as a transient non-place, it also offers a number of opportunities for resistance with authorities recognizing it is "a difficult space to police, and a space where criminals can slip away undetected" (160).

Crash positions itself in an interesting way in terms of the governance of the motorway and attempts by agencies to bring to light improper use. The characters of *Crash* utilise mobile space to realise a series of experiments that are often criminal in nature. The motorway offers them opportunities for resistance circulating around points of governmental concern precisely because it is a fluid and unfixed space. The car crash as undesirable performance within the space of the motorway is reconfigured by *Crash* as a locus point of resistance to the smooth running of non-place. The imaginative restaging of crashes enacted within the text disrupts governance and regulation, allowing a reinvestment in space. Early in the text, James Ballard visualises a series of subversive crashes:

> absurd deaths of the wounded, maimed and distraught. I think of the
> crashes of psychopaths, implausible accidents carried out with venom

and self-disgust, vicious multiple collisions contrived in stolen cars on evening freeways among tired office-workers. I think of the absurd crashes of neurasthenic housewives returning from their VD clinics, hitting parked cars in suburban high streets. I think of the crashes of excited schizophrenics colliding head-on into stalled laundry vans in one-way streets; of manic-depressives crushed while making pointless U-turns on motorway access roads; of luckless paranoids driving at full speed into the brick walls at the ends of known culs-de-sac; of sadistic charge nurses decapitated in inverted crashes on complex interchanges; of lesbian supermarket manageresses burning to death in the collapsed frames of their midget cars before the stoical eyes of middle-aged firemen; of autistic children crushed in rear-end collisions, their eyes less wounded in death; of buses filled with mental defectives drowning together stoically in roadside industrial canals.

C 7–8

The imagination of the crash opens fissures in the operation of non-place. James Ballard's fantasies uncover a series of disavowed events within the spaces of road and motorway. He imagines intentional crashes caused by people excluded by normative governmental authorities accessing space in deviant ways so that crashes become spatial extensions of their undesirability.

The text of *Crash* knowingly appropriates the event of the car crash as a hidden point of resistance by utilizing the same experimental techniques designed to make the motorway appear safe. The character of Dr Robert Vaughan, "nightmare angel of the expressways" (*C* 66) is also described as a "hoodlum scientist" (*C* 11), hiding his subversive actions beneath the veneer of investigative science. Meeting James Ballard for the first time he disguises himself as authority figures: first as a "white-coated doctor" (*C* 31) and then as "police photographer" (*C* 51). Vaughan's background in "the application of computerized techniques to the control of all international traffic systems" (*C* 48) shows up his knowledge of the kind of intervention designed to make the motorway into a regulated and predicable space. He is attracted to the Road Research Laboratory, an organization established by the UK government concerned with road safety, planning, and control, where he watches "calibrated vehicles crashing into [...] concrete target blocks" (*C* 3). Vaughan utilizes governmental techniques used to regulate and control the motorway space in order to produce his own results. He evaluates the event of the crash, preparing meticulous documentary evidence including questionnaires: "In each questionnaire the subject was given a list of celebrities from the world of politics, entertainment, sport, crime, science and the arts, and invited to devise an imaginary car-crash in which one of them might die" (*C* 107), which show "all the benefits of an exhaustive and lingering research" (*C* 107). This evidence is supplemented by a series of illustrating photographs "assembled with enormous care, torn from the pages of forensic medical journals and textbooks of plastic surgery, photocopied from internally circulated monographs, extracted from operating theatre reports stolen during his visits to Ashford Hospital" (*C* 108). Vaughan's cataloguing plays on governmental tactics of knowing, and arrays of technologies used to intervene in motorway space are subverted to become points of resistance designed to produce a radically different *connaissance* of the crash.

Whilst governmental understanding of the motorway effectively tries to avoid the improper event of the car accident, Vaughan's investigations linger over the crash subjecting it to perverse knowledge and understanding: "units in a new currency of pain and desire" (*C* 109). His repeated photographing of victims and wreckage is a further subversion of the systems of knowing applied by governing authorities:

> I looked down at the discarded prints below my feet. Most of them were crude frontal pictures of motor-cars and heavy vehicles involved in highway collisions, surrounded by spectators and police, and close-ups of impacted radiator grilles and windshields. Many had been taken by an unsteady hand from a moving car, showing the blurred outlines of angry police and ambulance attendants, remonstrating with the cameraman as he swerved past them.
>
> *C* 76

The act of photography captures and lingers over fleeting moments disavowed by the quick clearing away of debris, setting up a stubborn block within fluid road space, and the photograph is here used as a technology of resistance. Vaughan's photographs offer the possibility of reconfiguring the accident by utilizing its hidden recalcitrant traces: close-ups of impacted radiator grilles and windscreens disavowed by governing authorities. The pictures taken from a moving car defy authority, angering police and ambulance attendants, but the fluidity of the motorway allows Vaughan to swerve past them. Casting Vaughan as a Surrealist photographer, Baxter notes that by "isolating the detail of an event (a crushed door, a blood-soaked seat, an amputated limb), Surrealist photography functions to install moments of critical and historical reflection by bearing witness to that which threatens to pass unnoticed and undocumented" (131). Vaughan's documentary evidence is a reading of hidden detail written into the non-place of the motorway.

In *Crash*, the space of the motorway is accessed in a number of rebellious ways. As Merriman's study of the M1 motorway points out, driving on the motorway "is a complex *social* practice and activity, and drivers do communicate and interact with people and all manner of things, inhabiting and consuming the spaces of the car and road in a myriad of distinctive ways" (11). In particular: "The materiality of cars and vehicles is intimately entwined with the spaces, embodied actions, identities and subjectivities of *driving* (as well as simply *owning* a car), and it is important to recognize that there are clear differences between the experiences and embodied actions of drivers and passengers" (7). This postulates a kind of "'tight-coupling' or hybridisation of drivers and vehicles" (193); an embodied driving that appropriates the space of the motorway in original ways. This is an important observation as vehicles become vital in a process of identity formation as individualized extensions of their drivers in *Crash*. The type of car you dive, and how you drive, can enable an act of resistance. *Crash* describes a complex synthesis of the human and machine, and vehicles constantly mark their owners in physical ways. After his accident, the instrument panel and steering wheel imprint themselves on James Ballard to such a degree that an automobile engineer could predict the exact make and model of his car from his wounds (*C* 18).

Cars become extensions of their owners. Vaughan's car is described as dusty and dirty, and the way in which he aggressively drives his vehicle is an extension of personality: "The way Vaughan handled the car set the tone for all his behaviour – by turns aggressive, distracted, sensitive, clumsy, absorbed and brutal" (*C* 70). In opposition to governmental space, the motorway opens up the possibility of the circulation of resistant enclaves expressed through the materiality of the vehicle in the form of embodied driving. It is no surprise that Vaughan's car is dirty, its "dusty windows" (*C* 122) making the interior cabin space opaque to the outside gaze of authority. The importance of embodied driving in *Crash* explores the idea of the heterotopic enclave, and the enclosed site of the car cabin becomes a site of imaginative investment as a personalized locus of resistance. James Ballard describes the cabin of his car as "the perfect module for all the quickening futures of my life" (*C* 53). Throughout *Crash* it is turned into a heterotopia much like Foucault's motel room used for illicit sex. His lover, Helen Remington's car cabin is also transformed and expanded by imaginative investment: "In my mind I visualized the cabin of Helen's car, its hard chrome and vinyl, brought to life by my semen, transformed into a bower of exotic flowers, with creepers entwined across the roof light, the floor and seats lush with moist grass" (*C* 97). The cabin is a space marked by personal use, and semen and other corporeal fluids continually stain fabrics and plastics. The cabins of cars are never clean, and James Ballard notices evidence of prior use clinging to interiors:

Despite the efforts made to clean these cars, the residues of the previous drivers clung to their interiors – the heelmarks on the rubber mats below the driving pedals; a dry cigarette stub, stained with an unfashionable lipstick shade, trapped by a piece of chewing gum in the roof of the ash-tray; a complex of strange scratches, like the choreography of a frantic struggle, that covered the vinyl seat, as if two cripples had committed rape on each other.

    C 44

These residues trace the way in which interiors are appropriated by their own-ers defying sanctioned use. In particular, it is possible to trace evidence of sub-versive sexual acts taking place in car cabins as a form of rebellious social rule breaking.

Contained within the larger motorway space, the car cabin is a personalized space allowing the characters of *Crash* to open up the idea of a hidden hetero-topia that can be rebelliously established within the parameters of non-place. The cabin, physically marked by the presence of the owner, becomes an en-clave within the containing motorway. This is akin to a heterotopia of illusion, a site of imaginative possibility, established within an ordered heterotopia of compensation. It is a locus from which new possibilities can be imagined and experimented upon. The cabin enclave, surrounded by the materiality of the car, defies pronouncements about the correct use. Embodied driving becomes a way to defiantly access non-place, imprinting personality on to anonymous and impersonal spaces.

Sexual activity taking place within the car cabin is a hidden form of im-proper use that challenges the logics of governed motorway non-place. One vivid section of *Crash* depicts James Ballard voyeuristically observing his wife Catherine having sex with Vaughan in the back seat of his car going through a car-wash. The trip to the car-wash is necessitated by mysterious streaks of "black gelatinous material" (*C* 129) smeared across the nearside front wheel of the car, arousing the fear that the police will impound the car. The car-wash is therefore a way to evade the unwanted attention of the police, and James Bal-lard conspires with Vaughan to cover up their deviant access of the motorway space. The "all-night car-wash in the airport service area" (*C* 129) is a corollary of the non-place of the motorway where cars are cleaned day and night, en-suring their smooth functioning and proper appearance. In *Crash*, the space of the car-wash becomes an opportunity for concealment that at the same time absolves Vaughan by washing away incriminating evidence. On the jour-ney to the car-wash, James Ballard notices the "evening air was crossed by the navigation lights of airliners and maintenance vehicles, by the thousands of headlamps flowing along Western Avenue and the flyover" (*C* 130). This is a space of excessive illumination open to observation. In contrast, watching the car-wash, he sees a taxi going through the machine and the interior of the cabin is hidden by the rollers and soapy water so that the driver and his wife become "invisible and mysterious mannequins" (*C* 131) in a temporarily hidden enclave. Inside the car-wash, James Ballard watches Vaughan have sex with Catherine, an act which is described as "a stylized encounter between two bodies which recapitulated their sense of motion and collision" (*C* 132). Washing clean the outside of the car, and removing incriminating traces of blood, the car-wash covers the subversive coupling of Vaughan and Catherine. Ironically, the car-wash becomes a space that unearths rebellious sexual desire effectively hidden from view, and the car cabin is further obscured by machinery associated with cleanliness and transparency. A discourse of seeing is contrasted with concealment operating in apparently open and accessible space. The car cabin, inserted into non-place, becomes a space of resistance hidden from external gaze.

Crash coalesces around a central tension between discourses of seeing and not seeing. Against a discourse of seeing that attempts to open the space of the motorway to the light of knowledge and regulation, Ballard's text establishes a series of heterotopias of resistance. Hidden from authority as an unintentional accident, the car crash is appropriated as a rebellious act that knowingly subverts officially sanctioned uses of space. In particular, the character of Vaughan, hiding as an authority figure, carries out a series of idiosyncratic investigations utilising techniques of knowing appropriated from regulatory governmental interventions in motorway space. The car cabin becomes a hidden enclave where it is possible to imagine alternative spatial possibilities. Characters utilize the car-wash, machinery in the service of visibility designed to make things clean, to hide illicit activity. The subversive project of *Crash* is an attempt to recover hidden meaning. The text's appropriation of physical spaces, scientific discourse, and documentary evidence engenders resistance at precisely the points where authority attempts to intervene and regulate.

Hidden heterotopic enclaves are spaces where everything judged undesirable and disavowed in the creation of non-place can be recovered. Often these spaces are only briefly accessible, quickly shut down by the regulatory demands of non-place. The "extreme metaphor" (*C* vi) represented by the car crash functions as a transient heterotopic site. Placed under surveillance as an event that is incommensurable with the functioning of non-place, the crash cannot be effectively integrated within the space of the motorway and is therefore quickly cleared by anxious authorities. The actions of the rebellious subjects attempt to recover the crash as a sustained point of resistance.

Works Cited

Augé, Marc. *Non-Places: An Introduction to Supermodernity*. Translated by John Howe. London: Verso, 2008.

Baxter, Jeannette. *J.G. Ballard's Surrealist Imagination: Spectacular Authorship*. Farnham: Ashgate, 2009.

Boyer, M. Christine. "The Many Mirrors of Foucault and Their Architectural Reflections." In *Heterotopia and the City: Public Space in a Post-Civil Society*. Edited by Michiel Dehaene and Livien De Cauter. London: Routledge, 2008. 53–74.

Doron, Gil. "'…those marvellous empty zones on the edge of out cities': Heterotopia and the 'Dead Zone.'" In *Heterotopia and the City: Public Space in a Postcivil Society*. Edited by Michiel Dehaene and Lieven de Cauter. London: Routledge, 2008. 203–15.

Foucault, Michel. "Of Other Spaces." In *Heterotopia and the City: Public Space in a Postcivil Society*. Edited and translated by Michiel Dehaene and Lieven de Cauter. London: Routledge, 2008. 13–30.

Francis, Samuel. *The Psychological Fictions of J.G. Ballard*. London: Continuum, 2011.

Gasiorek, Andrzej. *J.G. Ballard*. Manchester: Manchester University Press, 2005.

Goron, Colin. "Governmental Rationality: An Introduction." In *The Foucault Effect: Studies in Governmentality*. Edited by Graham Burchell, Colin Gordon and Peter Miller. Chicago: University of Chicago, 1991. 1–52.

Groes, Sebastian. "The Texture of Modernity in J.G. Ballard's *Crash, Concrete Island* and *High-Rise*." In *J.G. Ballard: Visions and Revisions*. Edited by Jeannette Baxter and Rowland Wymer. London: Palgrave Macmillan, 2012. 123–141.

Hetherington, Kevin. *The Badlands of Modernity: Heterotopia and Social Ordering*. London: Routledge, 1997.

Luckhurst, Roger. *"The Angle Between Two Walls": The Fiction of J.G. Ballard*. Liverpool: Liverpool University Press, 1997.

Merriman, Peter. *Driving Spaces: A Cultural-Historical Geography of England's M1 Motorway*. Oxford: Blackwell, 2007.

Soja, Edward W. *Postmodern Geographies: The Reassertion of Space in Critical Social Theory*. London: Verso, 1989.

Stephenson, Gregory. *Out of the Night and into the Dream: A Thematic Study of the Fiction of J.G. Ballard*. London: Greenwood Press, 1991.

CHAPTER 9

Pillars of the Community: The Tripartite Characterization of *High-Rise*

William Fingleton

Abstract

This chapter examines the inter-relationships between the primary residents of Ballard's fictional tower, both in literal and symbolic terms. In *High-Rise*, the reader encounters a tower populated by what is initially described as "a virtually homogeneous collection of well-to-do professional people" (*HR* 10). As the narrative unfolds, the tenants demonstrate variations in characterization that constitute a unique literary experiment. The tripartite focalisation of *High-Rise* is emblematic of a widespread dementia as the perspectives of Wilder, Laing and Royal interweave and affect each other. Though each protagonist stands alone, they are explored as representations of Freud's cognitive model, as emblems of class consciousness, or as archetypal exemplars of the divergent conditions of pronoia, paranoia or metanoia.

Keywords

J.G. Ballard – *High-Rise* – psychogeography – post-Freudian – metanoia – identity – technology – devolution – haunted house – symbolism – Freud – R.D. Laing – Frederic Jameson

> The way out is via the door. Why is it that no-one will use this method?
> Confucius

In *Lost in Space: Geographies of Science Fiction*, Jonathon Taylor argues that "rather than stressing a sociological, political or psychological motivation, J. G. Ballard's vision is centred upon geography as both the expression and main agent of change in human subjectivity" (91). Ballard's texts have long demonstrated a link between psychic and physical landscapes as having a mutually affective relationship. *Hello America* (1981) and *The Day of Creation* (1987), for example, both deal macroscopically with this phenomenon, exploring the scenery of, respectively, America and Africa and their ability to invigorate/

repulse/blossom/waste, as appropriate. Ballard's *The Wind From Nowhere* (1961), *The Drowned World* (1962), *The Drought* (1965),*The Crystal World* (1966), and *Rushing to Paradise* (1994) all focus on the influence of extreme natural landscapes on the populace just as, dialectically, *Crash* (1973), *Concrete Island* (1974), and *High-Rise* (1975) explore, in finer detail, the ramifications of living in our technological modernity. *High-Rise* is therefore an extreme close-up of an extreme geography, the vertical city and its relationship with its dwellers. Here, the environment is shown to alter the inner perceptions of its residents while simultaneously operating as an outward manifestation of internal psychic processes.

In *High-Rise*, Ballard adopts a tripartite focalization to guide the reader through the fluctuating dynamics of his vertical village. This is atypical of an author who tends to centre his narratives on the perspective of a single protagonist, though it works well in this text as the story concerns the emergence of what Gregory Stephenson calls a "collective psychosis" (81). Not unlike the multiple aspects of the T character in *The Atrocity Exhibition* (1970), *High-Rise* explores the loosening grip on reality from several perspectives which may be viewed separately or collectively. Travis, Traven, Tallis, and so on, can be read as aspects of a single fractured identity, just as the protagonists of *High-Rise* are primarily emblematic of a generic social type. The characters of Robert Laing, Richard Wilder and Anthony Royal are representative of what is initially described as "a virtually homogenous collection of well-to-do professional people" (*HR* 10); upper-class dwellers of an affluent development by the banks of the Thames. As the narrative unfolds, it becomes apparent that these three men, despite their geographical similitude, are emblematic of philosophies divergent, contradictory and sometimes inseparable.

Wilder, who begins the novel as a dweller of the bottom levels, is portrayed as a brute, a titan, a man mountain; obsessed with his own physicality and need to dominate in corporeal terms. Ballard echoes the Atlas myth as he depicts a man burdened by the immense weight of the heavens/havens above him and his ultimate desire to wreak vengeance on the man he blames for that heft, the architect who lives like an Olympian in the tower's penthouse, Anthony Royal.

Wilder, initially motivated by professional curiosity, procures a cine-camera and begins an ascent of the high-rise in an effort to document the increasingly berserk territorial disputes that erupt throughout the building. He reinvents himself as a mountaineer, convinced of the righteousness of his cause. The mountain motif is synonymous with Wilder just as Laing and Royal have their own unique views on the building. The cragsman's basecamp lies in the foothills of the massif on the second floor. As the narrative unfolds, Wilder becomes obsessed with climbing the mountain in terms of a Herculean challenge.

Initially, we are led to believe that Wilder's lofty ambition corresponds to an ironic caricature of the notion of social climbing as higher levels denote a superior level of prestige. For instance, as Wilder reaches the 27th floor, we are told that "he felt like a well-to-do landowner who had just bought himself a mountain" (*HR* 116). His ascent is matched by a corresponding devolution. He replaces clothing with improvised body-paint, foregoing the power of speech "as if words introduced the wrong set of meanings into everything" (*HR* 130). Wilder's regression parallels the other residents of the building as the social structure devolves from order, through a feudal period to anarchy. As language and verbal communication break down throughout the building, there is an equivalent increase in graffiti, vandalism and violence as the dominant forms of expression.

As the novel draws toward its conclusion, Wilder's antipathy toward Royal is replaced by a childish misunderstanding of the nature of their relationship. When they meet in their final scene together, we see that "he [Wilder] was unsure whether Royal had come to play with him or reprimand him [...] Wilder waved his pistol playfully at Royal [...] the architect flinched back as is pretending to be frightened" (*HR* 166). There is a suggestion that Wilder's perceived "reprimand" intimates Royal as his real or imagined father. This is repeated through Wilder's seeming familiarity with the penthouse apartment, "almost expecting to find his childhood toys, a cot and a playpen laid out for his arrival" (*HR* 165). The Oedipal trajectory is realized through the younger man absentmindedly shooting his imagined father.

Shortly afterward, Wilder achieves his goal of reaching the rooftop, only to meet a group of cannibalistic women who he, again, confuses as allies. In a curious failure of recognition when looking at one woman, Wilder professes that "he recognized her as his wife, Judith" (*HR* 167). Wilder's inability to remember the correct name of his spouse may be indicative of a state of a certain type of blindness: the inability of the eyes and the memory to successfully communicate. This blindness serves to further sustain the Oedipal sub-text of Wilder's story arc, as in Sophocles' version of the myth, it is only after the realization that he has committed patricide that Oedipus blinds himself in an effort to purge the memory from his mind.

In Wilder's last act, as he moves toward the armed and hungry women we are told how "shy but happy now, Wilder tottered across the roof to meet his new mothers" (*HR* 168). His madness notwithstanding, Wilder reaches his finale in a state of childlike innocence – a transcendental release from the psychic pressures felt most emphatically at the base of the building having reached the tower's peak. To quote Warren Wagar and Martin Bax, "the whole point of [Ballard's] writing is to investigate how the 'hardware' of objects and environments affects the 'software' of human psyches" (53). In *High-Rise*, Wilder's decision to challenge and eventually dominate the structure which is the root of his mental strain results in a state of hard-won ecstasy that even negates the horror of his impending death. There is for Ballard, as Wagar emphasizes, "no path to nirvana or transcendence or utopia, except by running the gauntlet of the world"(53) or in this case, the high-rise.

Dr. Robert Laing, it has been noted by Peter Brigg amongst others, is likely to have taken his name from controversial psychiatrist R.D. Laing. The Scottish doctor is most famously remembered for his belief and practice within the Jungian concept of *metanoia*, that being:

> The idea that a psychotic breakdown is not a symptom of genetic abnormality or a neurological disorder, but an existential crisis; that is potentially a breakthrough to a more authentic and integrated way of being; and that professional and patient roles, as understood in mainstream psychiatry, are not conducive to the process of cure.
>
> Burston 77

Laing, at the beginning of the novel, admits to having moved into the high-rise to enjoy a state of anonymity following the tense dissolution of his marriage. Despite his hopes of inconspicuousness, Laing is in many ways the fulcrum of the novel, the liaison between the higher and lower residents made possible by both his role as a physician and also his geographical location on the 25th floor. Never depicted as aggressive as either Wilder or Royal, we are nevertheless given cues to Laing's psychic state as he views the London skyline visible from his own balcony as resembling "the disturbed encephalograph of an unresolved mental crisis" (*HR* 9). Further evidence of a deeper conflict within the doctor is hinted at by his references to his relationship with his sister, Alice, who also resides within the tower: "Even his sister's presence, and the reminders of their high-strung mother [...] seemed too close for comfort" (*HR* 13). Ballard, in a seeming nod to Freudian dynamic, includes information regarding Laing's early life just as Wilder's childhood is referenced. As other relations within the building alter, so too do the Laing siblings: "In the past he had always felt physically distanced from Alice by her close resemblance to their mother, but for reasons not entirely sexual this resemblance now aroused him" (*HR* 99).

In his professional life, Laing is represented as unambitious, preferring to avoid practicing medicine by continuing to teach at the nearby medical school. Similarly, his domestic habits – nude sunbathing and afternoon cocktails – also display a level of apathy that qualifies Robert Laing as the prototype for a new type of urban dweller in contrast to the primal natures of Wilder and other residents, "a cool, unemotional personality impervious to the psychological pressures of high-rise life" (*HR* 35). A further indicator of Laing's disconnectedness is evinced by his subservient nature in contrast to the two other central players. The doctor acquiesces to the more forceful wills of both his sadistic neighbour, Steele, and the informal leadership of the newscaster, Crosland, from the mid-levels which are contrary to the needs of both Wilder and Royal to dominate the building.

In line with his academic background, Laing is easily the most introspective of the main characters. He displays passivity and acceptance of the events unfolding within the high-rise, whilst simultaneously being fully conscious of the implications for the residents. At one of the many parties throughout the novel, Laing and Adrian Talbot, a colleague from the psychiatric department of the medical school, openly discuss the formation of the violent clan systems emerging in the tower without ever considering the possibility of relocation or intervention. In this way, Laing and the other residents are presented as a case study, just as Dr. Nathan, in *The Atrocity Exhibition*, outlines the parameters of the T-character's breakdown without proscribing any form of treatment. As Talbot explains to Laing:

> This building must have been a powerhouse of resentments – everyone's working off the most extraordinary backlog of infantile aggressions [...] It's a mistake to imagine that we're all moving towards a state of happy primitivism. The model here seems to be less the noble savage that our un-innocent post-Freudian selves, outraged by all that over-indulgent toilet-training, dedicated breast feeding and parental affection [...] Perhaps they resent never having had a chance to become perverse.
>
> *HR* 109

Talbot's analysis of the building's residents is paramount to understanding Ballard's underlying premise/joke. The irony of having the tower's residents as a "virtually homogenous" collective by the usual "educational and financial yardsticks" (*HR* 10) implies that it is precisely their privileged upbringing and exposure to psychodynamic theory that enables their subsequent devolution to the sort of primitivism described in works such as Freud's *Totem and Taboo*. Their behaviour is described as post-Freudian and therefore, coupled with the evidence of our doctor's surname, is likely designed to be regarded in Laingian terms – what Colin Greenland describes as "the Laingian reversal of delusion and common sense" (Greenland 119).

Greenland is referring to Ballard's ability to render stories of "psychic fulfilment" where, by any other measure, the protagonist would have been assessed

as the victim of a "galloping psychosis"(Greenland 119). This is consistent with
R.D. Laing's work on metanoia wherein deviant behaviour is viewed as a natural side-effect of the mind's efforts to reconstitute itself into an "integrated way
of being" (Burston 77). With this in mind, it is possible to view the high-rise as
a reimagining of Laing's Kingsley Hall experiment, where a large property in
London was sourced as "a refuge for people trying to avoid mental hospitals"
(Burston 83). Though Laing's experiment was partially successful for some residents, the structure-less nature of his therapeutic utopia resulted in chaos and
anarchy. It was subsequently closed. This suggests an inherent impracticality
with the implementation of R.D. Laing's doctrine on a large scale, as does *High-
Rise*, in an excessively violent way.

In *High-Rise*, the professional analytic abilities of Laing and Talbot serve no
purpose but to inform the reader about possible motivations for the tenants'
behaviour. No effort is made to contact outside assistance or, out of intellectual
curiosity, to document the increasingly bizarre happenings. As the narrative
progresses, Laing is even seen dismantling the furnishings of his apartment
and prising away the floorboards of his wardrobe: "in this suitcase-sized cavity
he hid away his cheque-book and insurance policies, tax-returns and share cer-
tificates. Lastly he forced in his medical case" (*HR* 105). These actions are less
an effort to safeguard his valuables than to perform the function of effectively
burying his former identity, that of healer, instead adopting his true high-rise
persona: the cave-dweller.

Laing's view of the high-rise as a series of caves in a cliff face is consistent
with his worldview. He is, as already mentioned, seeking a place of solitude
and anonymity upon his arrival in the building. The doctor repeatedly looks
forward to a time when he can be alone in the tower, "an environment built,
not for man, but for man's absence" (*HR* 25). As the visage of the tower is altered by the residents, Laing transmutes the images to suit his own paradigms.
For instance, the vitriolic graffiti daubed on Talbot's walls is described as being
"like the priapic figures drawn by cave-dwellers" (*HR* 108). Later, when electric-
ity fails on Laing's floor, the physician is unfazed and takes to cooking over
a phonebook-fuelled fire, kindled on his balcony; a perfect picture of Cro-
Magnon adaptation.

Laing's cave imagery is synonymous with Jung's archetypal symbolism,
wherein the cave is representative of a womb-like sanctum.[1] The confused feel-
ings the doctor experiences around his sister are later reconciled by his adop-
tion/abduction of both Alice and another neighbour, Eleanor Powell, to the

---

1 Jung's archetypal imagery is discussed in more detail in C.G. Jung, *The Archetypes and The
   Collective Unconscious.*

sanctity of his lightless apartment. This outcome is not presented as a chance occurrence as Laing earlier expresses his desire to "build his dwelling place where he was, with this woman [Alice] and in this cave in the cliff face" (*HR* 99).

Toward the end of the novel, Laing, like Wilder, has achieved a state of relative nirvana. The living arrangement the doctor has designed sees Laing, his sister and Eleanor existing in a curious symbiosis: the physician provides for their physical survival as the two women remain bedridden and they, in turn, provide for the doctor's need to be dominated, in appearance at least. The relationship is akin to that between dominatrix and masochist. Laing describes the scenario as a "loosely evolving pantomime, treating him like two governesses in a rich man's ménage, teasing a wayward and introspective child" (*HR* 172).

Like Wilder, Laing regresses to a semi-childlike state when invoking terms such as "pantomime" and "governess." However, Laing's innocence is a ruse to disguise the callous and sinister possibilities which he wishes to explore with his houseguests: incest and forced morphine addiction are alluded to. It is, perhaps, Laing's callous streak which enables him to be the only survivor of the three main players at the close of the novel. However, as his feigned subservience to Alice and Eleanor prevents Laing's death from a band of marauding women, perhaps it would be fairer to suggest that it is the doctor's imagination that ultimately emancipates him, free to explore "what wayward impulses he gave way to, or which perverse pathways he chose to follow" (*HR* 172). In this way, Laing epitomizes the metanoic credo of his namesake and continues as proof of its possible, though arguable, benefits.

Anthony Royal, architect of the high-rise, is the most contrary of the main characters. Both his name and station indicate a privileged background, though as we learn, Royal has married into wealth rather than earned or, as his surname suggests, inherited his status. His nouveau-riche sensibilities are just one facet of the many variables that contribute to Royal's cognitive dissonance. In appearance, Royal is described as tall, thin, long-haired, wearing a white jacket and accompanied by his white Alsatian. Replacing his dog with an alligator, one may find an uncanny resemblance between Royal and an earlier Ballardian character, "The Man with the White Smile" Strangman, from *The Drowned World* (*DW* 90). Strangman is portrayed as the villain, primarily due to his failure to recognize the psychological devolution triggered by the radically altered environment presented within that text. Furthermore, Strangman clings to an obsolete materialism that has been superseded for the other characters by the need to adapt to their transformed *archeopsychic*[2] selves. Similarly, within

---

2   "Archeopsychic" is a term taken from *The Drowned World* (1962), acknowledging the many millennia of evolution and genetic inheritance which create the brain that we refer to as

High-Rise, Royal frequently misjudges his own position, both in relation to how he is perceived and also his contribution to the tower in which he lives.

Both Strangman and Royal imagine affinities with great swarms of animals. In *The Drowned World*, Strangman's arrival is heralded by the huge congregation of alligators which his crew has ensnared. This "massive incarnation of reptilian evil" (*DW* 87) is symbolic, designed to denote Strangman's unscrupulous motives. The disloyal and dangerous alligators are a fitting metaphor for Strangman himself. Royal, on the other hand, first gathers a pack of dogs to himself and later, abandons all but his white Alsatian to pursue his imagined affinity with the seagulls which inhabit the roof. Royal's uncertainty as to which animal best suits his own persona is indicative of a deeper uncertainty regarding his own motivations and, therefore, is comparable to Strangman's failure to identify with the corresponding changes in the larger environment. As we have witnessed Wilder's adaptation to be instinctually physical and Laing's to be a willing submission to the unfolding transformation, Royal's adaptation is uncertain at best.

The genesis of Anthony Royal's vacillation seems to stem from his relationship with the tower itself. As contributing architect and first tenant of the tower, Royal's connection with the building seems especially synchronous, particularly regarding the degenerative physical condition of either. We are told that Royal's work on the building "sadly for him had concerned those very sections which had borne the brunt of the resident's hostility" (*HR* 69). Royal's pre-narrative car accident seems to have occurred at an unspecified but crucial juncture in the construction of the high-rise. Ballard implies a deeper connection between the damage sustained by the architect and a parallel anthropomorphic corruption of the building. Evidence of this association may be found as a despondent Royal, in his opening chapter, describes how "this huge building he had helped to design was moribund, its vital functions failing one by one [...] As if in sympathy, the old injuries to his legs and back had begun to keen again" (*HR* 68). As time goes on, Royal's integration with the tower is transferred to the residents, whose burgeoning primal energies reinvigorate the architect's own dynamism: "Each one bringing his invisible tribute to Royal's well-being" (*HR* 73). Anthony Royal, therefore, is shown to have an antagonistic, yet symbiotic, relationship with the other tenants of the block; he is at once the symbol of the building's failings, though simultaneously, inadvertent developer of what he sees in his most conceited moments as "a pattern of social organization that would become the paradigm of all future high-rise blocks [...] their new Jerusalem" (*HR* 70).

---

modern.

Royal's relationships with those closest to him are as undecided as his own with the building. At the opening of the novel, Laing and Royal are weekly squash partners only for the architect to abruptly sever his ties with the doctor. Likewise, Wilder's initial *ressentiment*[3] toward the designer is, as already noted, replaced by an imaginary patricide. The architect's unfaithful wife later shares him with her friend, then abandons him when Royal loses his status as clan-leader of the upper levels. After this he adopts and loses Wilder's wife only to repeat the process with his dogs. Eventually, Royal turns his attentions to the seagulls, which may be an attempt at acknowledging his continually repressed guilt in an urban salute to *The Rime of The Ancient Mariner's* albatross motif. He wonders, "Perhaps they identified him as one of their own, a crippled old albatross who had taken refuge on this remote roof-top beside the river" (*HR* 79). In an insightful moment of reflection, Royal muses that "he had come up in the world, all right, in too many senses of the term. In an insane way his [car] accident might have been an attempt to break out of the trap" (*HR* 74). This admission points to a latent fatalism that explains the continuing failure of his relationships and his ultimate desire to die within the boundaries of his own immense mausoleum.

Royal's white safari-jacket and matching Alsatian become elements of a the-atricality used to cow his neighbours. After an altercation, Royal smears his jacket with the fresh blood of his wounded dog and stalks the building using the carmine streaked garment and hound as an aggressive decalcomania, a vi-sual statement both of betrayal and hostile intent. This act serves to further distinguish the variant characters of the tower's main tenants. Laing, for in-stance, never employs war-paint as a symbol, preferring instead to immerse himself within the natural unhygienic deterioration of his own body, his own scents in harmony with the general atrophy of the high-rise. Wilder directly applies emulsion to his skin, in line with his feral integration with the building's growing primitivism. Royal, however, neither displays his own colours nor goes fully native as Wilder does. Instead, the architect paints only his jacket with the dog's blood, an act which disguises his own pheromonal cues while coming off as half-baked, lacking the commitment of Wilder's primeval communique.

Royal's theatricality extends to the lavish dinners prepared on the top levels long after the rest of the tower has devolved past such rituals. These dinners further indicate Royal's failure to properly engage with the pervading mood of the high-rise. As we hear:

---

3   "*Ressentiment*" is used here as a psychological term similar in meaning to the more common resentment, though with connotations of use as an ego-defence mechanism. Gasiorek uses the term in his appraisal of Wilder's character (Gasiorek 126).

> The one error that Royal and Pangbourne had made was to assume that there would always be some kind of social organization below them which they could exploit and master [...] The clans had broken down into small groups of killers [and] solitary hunters.
>
> *HR* 133

When Royal finally recognizes the altered reality of the high-rise, he attributes the cause to his own unconscious desire to create "a giant vertical zoo [...] All the events of the past few months made sense if one realized that that these brilliant and exotic creatures had learned to open the doors" (*HR* 134). As Gasiorek observes, Royal's mystification of the building's residents as "brilliant creatures" (127) cloaks a denial that the habitat which the architect has created is an utter failure, one in which not even its designer can live with.

Royal's last days are spent alone with only his Alsatian and his psychosis for company. His obsession with the circling gulls escalates to the stage where he "was certain now that they were calling for him" (*HR* 162), thereby declining to recognize the repeating patterns of abandonment and isolationism within the building. Curiously, and perhaps an indication of the unsuccessfulness to which Royal adapts to the tower's metamorphosis, the architect's final moments are only related to us from the perspectives of the other main protagonists. Wilder, as we have already witnessed, shoots Royal in a confused state of childlike madness and in a chapter entirely focalized from the mountaineer's perspective. Later, Laing relates the conclusion of the architect's life, after he has painfully made his way down to the 10th floor concourse. At the end, the bloodstains which paint the architect's jacket are his own: "as if he had tried to identify himself with these imprints of his own death to come" (*HR* 170). Royal is last sighted entering the mass-grave which the drained swimming-pool had now become, perhaps in a belated act of solidarity with his neighbours.

Ballard's high-rise is, depending on the character's viewpoint, a cave, a mountain, a zoo and, for all, a prison. Its vastness enables a variety of interpretations that constitute multiple translations of a space which is designed as, though almost never referred to, as a home. This suggests that, for the author at least, the concept of the high-rise is flawed and ultimately alienating for those who live there. In Ballard's novel, the high-rise is a naturalistic environment that triggers unnatural behaviours in the dwellers of that building. Here, we negotiate a bridge between architecture and psychology. In this sense, *High-Rise* may be viewed as a modern reimagining of the gothic haunted house motif. As Fredric Jameson observes in *The Cultural Turn*:

The ghost story is indeed virtually the architectural genre par excellence, wedded as it is to rooms and buildings ineradicably stained with the memory of gruesome events, material structures in which the past literally weighs like a nightmare on the brain of the living. (187)

Ballard's narrative is a story rooted in a modern architectural construct and, therefore, lacking the "memory" associated with gothic architecture. As Jameson admits, "one scarcely associates ghosts with high-rise buildings" (188). Yet, the narrative presents a building that exhibits an observable presence in passages where one resident "referred to the high-rise as if it were some kind of huge animate presence, brooding over them and keeping a magisterial eye on the events taking place" (*HR* 40), or where "an almost palpable miasma hung over the [swimming pool], as if the spirit of the drowned beast was gathering to itself all the forces of revenge and retribution present within the building" (*HR* 22). Even the enormous body count at the conclusion of *High-Rise* seems in line with an industrial reimagining of the haunted house motif, the bodies stacked in the 10th floor swimming pool akin to some sort of economical revision of a spirits-per-square-metre formulation in lieu of the building's immensity. In this way, the modern space is reconfigured as an updated superstition. As Jon Savage has remarked, "High-Rise blocks are very compelling pieces of architecture [...] the City of London looks like a graveyard, the tall office buildings look like tombstones" (*EM* 113).

As the haunted house genre plays on the fears of the unknown, the arcane and the superstitious, so Ballard inverts the mythology, presenting an ultra-modern living space which nevertheless manifests horrors and deviant behaviours among the people living within. Ballard's premise is formed from the conceit of modernity in which society has debunked the forces of the supernatural through scientific enlightenment. In Ballard's view, the supernatural was never the worry, rather the infinitely more daunting natural, i.e. the dark and complex recesses of our own natures, where demons truly dwell.

Viewing *High-Rise* in terms of psychological symbolism, therefore, we may notice alternative aspects of the author's intent. In his own study of this novel, Andrzej Gasiorek observes how the tenant's "personalities [are] created and shaped by the id-like building itself" (125). This analysis conforms to Freud's spatial model of the human psyche denoting the tower as representative of the subconscious drives which would explain, in psycho-geographical terms, how all the tenants are simultaneously affected by such a mass outbreak of dementia. An alternative interpretation would be to view the variant protagonists as symbolically emblematic of Freud's mental triumvirate: Wilder as id, Royal as ego and Laing as superego.[4] Wilder readily occupies the id position given his easy surrender to the basest drives, as illustrated by his needs to fight, conquer and rape, coupled with his loss of linguistic faculty. Superego, formed by prevailing social etiquette, is personified by Laing and his quick acquiescence to the building's changeable norms and hierarchies. Royal, then, is left as the epitome of the ego, denoted by his unrealistic self-regard and cognitive dissonance. In this reading, it is necessary to understand and interrelate all three protagonists in order to comprehend the story as a functioning whole, just as Freud's mind-map signifies the id, ego and superego to form an integrated identity. However, this narrative integrates variant identities rather than a sole narrator. This demonstrates a model based on Freudian dynamic but incorporating a contextual element closer to the theories proposed by R.D. Laing:

> A person's 'own' identity cannot be completely abstracted from his identity-for-others. His identity-for-himself; the identity others ascribe to him; the identities he attributes to them; the identity or identities he thinks they attribute to him; what he thinks they think he thinks they think. (86)

In yet another way to read *High-Rise*, the three principal characters could be viewed as exemplars of divergent neuroses rather than Freudian schemata. Again drawing on R.D. Laing's already mentioned exploration of *metanoia*, we may ascribe that diagnosis to the doctor's namesake, in turn accrediting the appropriate states of *paranoia* to Anthony Royal and *pronoia*[5] to Richard Wilder. Laing's acceptance of his own breakdown is already well documented within this analysis and, in the text, never more explicit than in the final, chilling chapter in which he muses how "on the whole, life in the high-rise had been kind to him" or how the doctor felt "he owed the architect a debt of gratitude for having helped [...] make all this possible" (*HR* 173). Royal and Wilder contrastingly occupy two opposing extremes of an on-going set of dialectics through the novel: high/low, rich/poor(ish), slim/muscled, zoo-keeper/animal, cuckold/philanderer and so on. In keeping with this device, Ballard seems to set both men as psychical opposites; Wilder seemingly in the belief that his ascent to the summit is somehow ordained, and is finally so delusional as to

---

4 In "Reading Posture and Gesture in Ballard's Novels," Dan O'Hara notes a similar observance of Freud's mental triumvirate though with Royal in the super-ego role and Laing in the position of the ego.

5 "Pronoia" is a neologism which describes an opposite state to that of paranoia, where the individual believes in a conspiracy working to their benefit.

regard his murderers as "new mothers"; Royal, conversely, abandoned by all his one-time allies and easily tricked with an imagined threat (HR 143).

Whether pro- or paranoid, neither Wilder nor Royal survive the high-rise and, for Laing, we know his survival to be dependent on the marauding women "assuming him to be Eleanor's and Alice's prisoner" (HR 172). Indeed, apart from Robert Laing, the reader is told of no other man to survive the upheavals within the tower. Ballard may be suggesting that, contrary to the horde-father model proposed by Freud in *Group Psychology and The Analysis of The Ego*, in a post-Freudian world an organized society may not conform to previously established social structures, even when those societies devolve to a primal level. In the narrative, a late formed matriarchy is the last surviving social group and there is evidence in the text that suggests that this tribe will eventually reclaim the building. Just before his death, Wilder notices how

> A recent attempt had been made at house-keeping. The garbage sacks had been removed, the barricades dismantled, the lobby furniture reinstalled. Someone had scrubbed the walls, clearing away all traces of the graffiti.
>
> HR 165

As no-one else remained on the top floor, except the surviving children and their "new mothers," we must assume that Ballard purposefully uses this last-clan-standing motif, as Laing, in an echo of earlier events, simultaneously notices the adjacent tower achieving critical mass.[6] The author seems to suggest that while the calamity experienced within this block is destined to be repeated within the neighbouring one, these murderous events may not signify the end of the story. In this light, we may re-examine the significance of the seagulls which Royal had wrongly imagined as his own totemic animals. Seagulls have historically been viewed by sailors as associated with proximity to land and salvation. Being nesting creatures we may also draw an obvious parallel between the nesting habits of the gulls and the homely improvements carried out by the matriarchy on the 40th floor. The image of the gulls may

---

6   Critical mass is a term used by Wilder in *High-Rise* to describe the apartment block having reached full occupancy. While the term is commonly associated with the tipping point of a nuclear reaction, it is also used in the field of sociodynamics to describe the adoption of a social innovation adoption. Both interpretations could be used as a fitting metaphor for the mass outbreak of insanity described in Ballard's novel. More detail on the sociodynamic model may be found in Everett Rogers, *Diffusion of Innovations* (London: Simon & Schuster, 2003).

therefore be reinterpreted as a hopeful augury that life within the high-rise may continue under the reorganized guise of a post-Freudian sorority. This is not to suggest that such a sorority would be the natural outcome for the nearby building but rather that many different social structures could be generated from "the limitless possibilities of the high-rise" (*HR* 154).

The mundane space of the high-rise is merely one of the nodes of modernity which Ballard explores as a potential staging ground for a *sub rosa* revolution. In Laing, Wilder & Royal, Ballard invents the perspective agents of change. As the collective imagination further annexes the landscape around us and, in turn, alters the values and perceptions of the public, who can say what social types may spring forth from the generic nowheres of the world's motorways, business parks and shopping malls?

Works Cited

Brigg, Peter. *J.G. Ballard*. Mercer Island, WA: Starmont House, 1985.

Burston, Daniel. *The Wings of Madness: the Life and Work of R.D. Laing*. Cambridge: Harvard University Press, 1996.

Freud, Sigmund. *Beyond the Pleasure Principle, Group Psychology and Other Works*. London: Vintage, 2001.

Freud, Sigmund. *Totem and Taboo: Some Points of Agreement Between the Mental Lives of Savages and Neurotics*. London: Routledge & Keegan Paul, 1950.

Freud, Sigmund. *Group Psychology and The Analysis of The Ego*. Web. 28 September 2015.

Gasiorek, Andrzej. *J. G. Ballard*. Manchester: Manchester University Press, 2005.

Greenland, Colin. *The Entropy Exhibition*. London: Routledge & Keegan Paul, 1983.

Jameson, Fredric. *The Cultural Turn: Selected Writings on the Postmodern, 1983–1998*. London, Verso, 2009.

Jung, C.G. *The Archetypes and The Collective Unconscious*, 2nd Edition. London: Routledge, 1991.

Kerenyi, C. *The Gods of The Greeks*. Trans. Norman Cameron. Yugoslavia: Thames & Hudson, 1988.

Laing, R.D. *Self and Others*. London: Penguin Books, 1990.

O'Hara, Dan. "Reading Posture and Gesture in Ballard's Novels." *J.G. Ballard: Visions and Revisions*. Edited by Jeannette Baxter and Rowland Wymer. London: Palgrave Macmillan, 2012. 105–118.

Rogers, Everett. *Diffusion of Innovations*. London: Simon & Schuster, 2003.

Savage, Jon "J.G. Ballard" in *EM*. 106–120.

Sophocles. *Sophocles. Ajax, Electra, Oedipus Tyrannus*. Edited and translated by Lloyd-Jones Hugh. Vol. 1. Cambridge: Harvard University Press, 1994.

Stephenson, Gregory. *Out of the Night and into the Dream: A Thematic Study of the Fictions of J. G. Ballard.* Westport, CT: Greenwood Press, 1991.

Taylor, Jonathon S. "The Subjectivity of the Near Future: Geographical Imaginings in the Work of J. G. Ballard." *Lost in Space: Geographies of Science Fiction.* Edited by Kitchin, Rob and Kneale, James. London: Continuum, 2002. 90–103.

Wagar, Warren W. "J. G. Ballard and the Transvaluation of Utopia." *Science Fiction Studies* 18.1 (1991): 53–70.

CHAPTER 10

Fascisms and the Politics of Nowhere in *Kingdom Come*

Jeannette Baxter

Abstract

Focussing on *Kingdom Come*, this chapter explores how Ballard takes up the Surrealist "nowhere" motif in order to interrogate the survival of fascisms in contemporary history, politics and culture. With reference to Giorgio De Chirico's "The Disquieting Muses" and his little-known novel, *Hebdomeros*, I trace the aesthetic and political significances of De Chirico's enigmatic "nowhere" landscapes and his counter-political art of analogy for Ballard before interrogating how fascisms return in modified forms in Ballard's contemporary nowhere, from the soft-totalitarianism forged by the illusion of consumerist choice, to the neo-fascist communities that commit racially-motivated acts of violence against displaced, immigrant workers.

Keywords

J.G. Ballard – fascisms – Surrealism – De Chirico – nowhere – counter-politics – analogy – utopia – non-place – consumerism

> Ballard's achievement is not to have staked out any kind of political position
>
> JOHN GRAY, "Modernity and its Discontents."

John Gray's take on the political nature of Ballard's writing is a useful starting point for this discussion. Just as Ballard's novels and short stories offer determined resistance to official narratives of post-war history and culture, so they challenge totalizing political narratives with their prescriptive models of progress and change. *The Atrocity Exhibition* (1970) is probably the most sustained example of this. Across its fifteen disjointed texts, fragments of real-world political ideologies and systems are brought into chaotic relation with one another: European fascisms; National Socialism; American post-war and Cold War liberalism; Marxism and Communism; Environmentalism; U.S.

Conservatism; Anarchism; Socialism; and Political Capitalism (to name just a few). Far from being apolitical, as some early critics such as Finkelstein, Franklin and Stephenson maintained, Ballard's writings are better understood as counter-political in impulse; that is, they expose the inevitable limitations of totalizing political narratives whilst interrogating the complex structures and dynamics that shape and energize them.

Here, I explore the counter-political nature of Ballard's final novel *Kingdom Come* (2006), focusing specifically on its interrogation of fascisms in post-millennial culture and society. *Kingdom Come* is a valuable and timely counter-political text for at least two related reasons. Firstly, it challenges conventional understandings of fascism as a totalizing political ideology that was overcome at the end of the Second World War. In this respect, Ballard's thinking chimes with that of contemporary historians and political scientists who insist that fascism should not be regarded from a safe historical distance, or as "an event that can ever be reduced to a discrete time period or state, society and culture" (Evans and Reid 2). As I will go on to show, *Kingdom Come* makes a disquieting case for the persistence of fascisms and, in so doing, it raises important questions about the interpenetration of power, violence and desire across contemporary political and cultural landscapes.

Secondly, *Kingdom Come* is alive to the mutable nature of fascisms across the twentieth and twenty-first centuries. As Roger Griffin puts it, fascisms are constantly on the move, transforming in nature and appearance as they adapt "to the unfolding conditions of modernity" (1). *Kingdom Come* keeps an extremely close eye to new manifestations of fascism, I suggest, tracking and interrogating at least five different models. They are: historical fascism, which denotes inter-war European fascisms in Italy, Germany and Great Britain; neo-fascism, which refers to post-war and contemporary fascist groups, such as the National Front, British National Party, and English Defence League; consumer fascism (or soft fascism), which is, for Ballard, the idea that consumerism is a form of fascism; "fascism," which speaks to the cultural production of fascism in literature, film and television; and micro-fascism, a model that turns away from an understanding of fascism as a historical regime or ideology in order to suggest that fascism is elementary not just to political life, but to everyday life itself. As Michel Foucault observed in his unnerving Preface to Gilles Deleuze and Félix Guattari's *Anti-Oedipus: Capitalism and Schizophrenia*: "Fascism is in us all, in our heads, and in our everyday behaviour" (xvii).

Throughout *Kingdom Come*, these five models of fascism co-exist in complex and dynamic ways, resisting any straightforward explanation or response. I therefore want to organize my discussion around Ballard's appropriation of the Surrealist motif of "nowhere." The Surrealist imagination has long protested against fascisms in visual, literary and non-fictional forms from the 1930s onwards, and artists and writers have consistently turned to the motif of nowhere to engage with the totalizing and deracinating forces of fascism and its attendant narratives of geo-political displacement and exile. We see this, for instance, in the work and activities of the Surrealist interwar anti-fascist group, *Contre-Attaque* (led by Georges Bataille and André Breton), and in interwar and wartime art and literature produced by the likes of Max Ernst, André Masson and Marcel Duchamp, all of whom were responding to Surrealism's artistic and political out-of-place-ness within a fascist Europe.

In the context of this discussion I particularly want to turn to the Italian artist and writer, Giorgio de Chirico. As is well documented, De Chirico's relationship with Surrealism was contentious and short lived. Having been instrumental in the foundation of Surrealism in Paris in the early 1920s, De Chirico was spectacularly banned from the Group in 1926 on the grounds of artistic treachery. The Italian artist's developing interests in neo-classical, baroque and romantic styles of painting were considered crimes against the revolutionary energies of artistic modernism. Nevertheless, De Chirico's enigmatic nowhere landscapes, in which displaced objects and faceless mannequins crowd unidentified piazzas, continued to exert a profound influence on Surrealist interrogations of time, memory and dreams. Consequently, four decades after the artist's official departure from Surrealism, Ballard went on to identify De Chirico as a key "iconographer of inner space" (*UGM* 200).

Indeed, De Chirico's enigmatic nowhere landscapes repeat with difference across the Ballardian imagination, and they emerge as particularly significant intertexts in *Kingdom Come*. Here, I limit myself to discussing just two: a painting, called "The Disquieting Muses" (1916–1919); and the little-known novel, *Hebdomeros* (1929). In my readings of these intertexts, I highlight two conspicuous but related features: firstly, the composite nowhere settings of each text; and secondly, De Chirico's technique of analogy. Specifically, I want to explore the poetics and politics of De Chirico's analogous nowheres for the ways in which they challenge fascist notions of national, cultural and artistic purity. Impurity was a consistent feature of De Chirico's artistic practice and political outlook, and it is this which has so much resonance for *Kingdom Come*. As I go on to argue, Ballard takes up and develops De Chirico's nowhere settings and his art of analogy in order to interrogate how and why fascisms survive within post-millennial culture. But this is not to suggest that *Kingdom Come* positions itself as a straightforward critique of the fascist imaginary. On the contrary, I explore Ballard's contemporary art of Surrealist analogy in order to venture the idea that *Kingdom Come* is an enigmatic text precisely because it does not strive to keep fascisms at a safe distance.

Nowhere and the Surrealist Imagination

De Chirico's nowhere landscapes have long shaped Ballard's Surrealist imagination. In "The Coming of the Unconscious" (1966), an essay that reads like a manifesto for post-war Surrealism, Ballard identifies "The Disquieting Muses" (1916–1918; see Figure 10.1) as one of six "key surrealist paintings":

> An undefined anxiety has begun to spread across the deserted square. The symmetry and regularity of the arcades conceal an intense inner violence; this is the face of catatonic withdrawal. The space within this painting, like the intervals within the arcades, contains an oppressive negative time. The smooth egg-shaped heads of the mannequins lack all features and organs of sense, but instead are marked with cryptic signs. These mannequins are human beings from whom all time has been eroded, and reduced to the essence of their own geometries.
>
> *UGM* 86

A striking feature of Ballard's description is his stress on what is either missing from, or not yet fully manifest in, De Chirico's landscape. Terms including

FIGURE 10.1
Giorgio de Chirico, Le Muse Inquietanti (The Disquieting Muses), *oil on canvas* (*1947*).

"undefined," "deserted," "conceal," "inner," "withdrawal," "negative time," "lack," "eroded," "reduced" work collectively to capture De Chirico's art of enigma, one rich in suggestion and absence. We can, of course, add to Ballard's synopsis the conspicuous non-setting of the painting. With no named locality or set of geographical co-ordinates to orient us, the spectator is left to inhabit a nowhere landscape.

In many respects, "The Disquieting Muses" is a typical De Chirico nowhere. Even though the artist drew on models and memories of real cities, such as Munich, Rome and Ferrara, the visual landscapes he produced are composite and do not exist as such. Instead, real geographical locations repeat across De Chirico's canvases as echoes that are inscribed in an analogous relationship with one another and with the Surrealist versions of themselves. This is because what matters for De Chirico, and for Ballard in his reading and appropriation of this painting, are the unexpected associations that analogous landscapes encourage between diverse geographies, cultures and experiences. As Keala Jewell observes, the "controversies related to the rise of modern nationalist cultures and ideologies were [...] ever present" (9) in the work of De Chirico. With the coming to power of Italian Fascism after the First World War, Italy was involved in discussions about how to think of itself as part of a "New Europe," one that was supposed to separate itself off from what was disparagingly called "'Eurasia'" (Jewell 9).

In contrast to fascist visions of the Italian nation as ordered, disciplined and pure in heritage, De Chirico understood Italy as "the most 'multiplicitous' and heterogeneous of places, possessed of rich layers of cultures: Greek, Roman, Christian, and modern" (Jewell 10). Therefore, De Chirico's analogous nowhere landscapes offered up something of a challenge to fascist claims to national purity whilst also resisting what Bataille had termed the "monstrous universal" of fascism; that is, fascism as a totalizing force that reduced a multiplicity of European nations and their cultures to a "state of empty shadows" (171) to a "NOWHERE" (173). In contrast to the monstrous universal of fascism, De Chirico's analogous nowheres advanced visions of Europe and, within that, Italy, as culturally replete, diverse and unbounded. It is hardly surprising, then, that De Chirico not only suffered "discriminatory treatment by the organizers of state-sponsored exhibitions that tended to exalt the nation," but he was also accused of unpatriotic "internationalism" (Jewell 7) by fascist ideologues.

In *Kingdom Come*, Ballard takes up the nowhere motif as part of his Surrealist engagement with fascisms. We first encounter Richard Pearson, a middle-aged advertising executive, travelling through a series of nowhere towns on his way to Brooklands, which is, we are told, another kind of nowhere place, being situated somewhere "between Weybridge and Woking" (*KC* 4), but which "seems to be off all the maps" (*KC* 6). In Ballard's post-millennial nowhere, however, it is not the monstrous universal of historical fascism that threatens to eradicate culture and community, but the monstrous universal of consumerism. This is how Geoffrey Fairfax, the resident solicitor and apparent defender of community and culture, puts it:

> Here in Brooklands we had a real community, not just a population of cash tills. Now it's gone, vanished overnight when that money-factory opened. We're swamped by outsiders, thousands of them with nothing larger on their minds than the next bargain sale" [...] He lowered his voice, as if the shadows in the deserted square might hear him. "Look around you, Mr Pearson. We're facing a new kind of man and woman – narrow-eyed, passive, clutching their store cards [...] This is a plague area, Mr Pearson. A plague called consumerism.
>
> *KC* 32–33

The intertextual nod to De Chirico's shadowy, partially-deserted piazza is conspicuous, serving most obviously to create analogies between his and Ballard's composite nowhere landscapes. In "The Disquieting Muses," for instance, the money-factories are symbolized by the modern factory buildings that creep up on the classical architectures of the Italian piazza (see Figure 1). In *Kingdom Come*, the money factory is the Metro-Centre, a vast and faceless shopping mall, which is yet another kind of analogous nowhere, being loosely modelled on the Bentall Shopping Centre in Kingston and the Bluewater Centre in Kent, and being an imaginary Ballardian nowhere. When discussing *Kingdom Come* with the novelist Toby Litt, Ballard revealed the importance of the novel's non-setting: "I wanted somewhere that didn't really exist" (*EM* 423). Of course, what particularly matters in Ballard's Surrealist critique of contemporary consumer-capitalism is that the analogous nowhere of *Kingdom Come* is composed of partially identifiable somewheres that can, in fact, be anywhere because, as Roger Luckhurst observes, Ballard's motorway towns are so "weirdly detached from an embedded culture or history or morality" (133).

   Luckhurst's comments are useful for opening up at least two other ways of thinking about the Metro-Centre as a kind of nowhere. Firstly, it is an example of what Marc Augé has termed a non-place. Shopping malls, airports and motorways are all examples of non-places because these phenomena of late-capitalism are transient spaces dedicated to consumption and exchange: "The habitué of supermarkets, slot machines and credit cards communicates wordlessly, through gestures, with an abstract, unmediated commerce" (Augé 78). Even though, for Augé, non-places are so called because they do not hold enough significance to be regarded as places (which are rich in history, community and diverse human experience), they are, nevertheless, sites of potential as the routes taken by the itinerant traveller loosen him or her from the roots of place and the authority of history and ideology. This critical ambivalence (Augé resists nostalgia for the past) has particular resonance for *Kingdom Come*. As David James observes, the transient characters of *Kingdom Come* are not in the least bit bothered about preserving a sense of community at Brooklands: "The more sinister condition, as Ballard implies, is revealed by the way a population can become entirely unperturbed, spending their money and leisure time together so seamlessly as to no longer require any individual reflection about what they're doing" (168).

The second way in which the Metro-Centre can be considered a nowhere place refers to Ballard's conspicuous recasting of the shopping mall as a form of consumerist utopia: coming from the Greek, utopia means no-place, a place in which time, space, memory and history are all absent. At numerous points throughout *Kingdom Come*, Ballard stresses the utopian spirit of the Metro-Centre with its privileging of shiny consumerist surface over any sense of experiential depth: "Death had no place in the Metro-Centre, which had abolished time and the seasons, past and future" (*KC* 40). For the authorities at the Metro-Centre, the shooting of Pearson's father is far more of an embarrassing blot on an otherwise spotless capitalist landscape than a human tragedy. Even the CCTV footage of the shooting incident (surely vital evidence) is cleaned-up for consumption: "Spilled shopping bags, scattered groceries, a screaming three-year-old with a blood-smeared face were all cropped and consigned to that vast amnesia that the consumer world reserved for the past [...] there were no yesterdays, no history to be relived, only an intense transactional present" (*KC* 46). Of course, what soon becomes clear in Ballard's re-fashioning of utopian space is that the Metro-Centre is a "special kind of nightmare utopia," one in which inconvenient histories are erased so that there are "fewer and fewer moral decisions to make" (Ballard "*Kingdom Come*: An Interview with J. G. Ballard" 124).

Contrary to Pearson's original impression, then, the Metro-Centre reveals itself to be anything but a benign shopping mall. This composite nowhere place is a nightmare utopia in which racist violence emerges as a way of alleviating the boredom of shopping. As Dr. Maxted, the resident psychologist, observes:

> Nasty things are brewing here. All this racism and violence [...] You've seen the people around here. Their lives are empty. Install a new kitchen, buy another car, take a trip to some beach hotel [...] People are bored [...]

> The danger is that consumerism will need something close to fascism in
> order to keep growing.
>
> KC 103–105

This passage connects two models of fascism at work in *Kingdom Come*: firstly,
consumer fascism, which is the basic idea that the totalizing dynamics of consumer capitalism operate as a form of fascism; secondly, neo-fascism, which
in Ballard's text is a form of racially-motivated violence born out of consumer
boredom. Rather intriguingly, a strand of reviewers, including Ursula Le Guin,
tended to read passages like this straight, and their response was to dismiss
Ballard's ideas as unrealistic and his mode of narration as "inadequate" and
"inconsistent [...] to the point of self-destruction" ("Revolution in the Aisles").

Pearson's narrative ambiguity is something to which I will return. For now,
it is worth noting Mike Holliday's re-assessment of fascism in *Kingdom Come*
because it is much more attuned to the dynamics of Ballard's literary Surrealism. Taking up Le Guin's and Harrison's damning reviews, Holliday suggests
that any realist readings of *Kingdom Come* are problematic for at least two
reasons. Firstly, he points out that if we read Ballard's novel straight, then the
"details fail to convince." Ballard's portrayal of ethnic minorities as antipathetic
to consumerism is a notable example. This detail not only seems unrealistic,
but it also "risks an accusation of racism because the novel implies that ethnic
minority groups are not interested in consumerism on the grounds of cultural
difference" (Holliday "Another Look at *Kingdom Come*"). Secondly, Holliday
argues that if *Kingdom Come* really is pushing the concept of consumer fascism, then it is asking us to make "an all-too-easy transition from 'totalizing'
to 'fascist,' a transition that effectively empties the term 'fascist' of meaningful
content and historical context" ("Another Look at *Kingdom Come*").

This is an important point because what fascism actually means is a constant preoccupation of *Kingdom Come*. When Sangster accuses Pearson of creating a fascist state through his "Mad is Bad. Bad is Good" advertising campaign
with David Cruise, Pearson responds like this: "Fascist?" I let the word hover
overhead, then dissipate like an empty cloud. "In the ... dinner party sense?"
[...] "Fascist? It's like 'new' or 'improved.' It can mean anything" (KC 167). In this
instance, Pearson's understanding of fascism belongs to the model of "fascism."
The quotation marks differentiate, as Petra Rau observes, historical fascism
from "fascism," with the latter referring to cultural productions of the former:
"Engaging 'fascism' is not the same as engaging *with* fascism; more often than
not, its citational practice [...] highlight[s] the desires we bring to 'fascism'" (4).
Indeed, Pearson's attraction to "fascism" and his knowledge of historical fascism are born out of at least one common source: his deceased father's library,

which is largely composed of coffee-table publications, including biographies of Juan Perón, Hermann Goering, Benito Mussolini, Adolf Hitler, and a history of Oswald Mosley and the British Union of Fascists. Pearson spends hours and hours poring over illustrated guides to Nazi regalia, the ceremonial uniforms of the Third Reich, and mass Nazi rallies. These glossy, visual histories of fascism are produced in order to fascinate, and Pearson even comments on the smell of the "coated paper that publishers seemed to reserve for atrocity photographs" (*KC* 193). He is also alert to the tiny "führer moustache and forelock on the spine of the Hitler biography" (*KC* 197): paratextual elements are all part of the package, ensuring that even the most cursory of glances at the spine of this book will draw the reader into the spectacle of "fascism."

But why are we so gripped by the Nazi era? Ballard has long engaged with this question, from "Alphabets of Unreason," the 1969 review of Hitler's *Mein Kampf* to "The Day of Reckoning," a 2005 review of Sebastian Heffner's *Germany: Jekyll and Hyde* and the anonymously published *A Woman in Berlin*. "The Day of Reckoning" is a sustained critique of contemporary cultural obsessions with the "spectral glamour of the Nazi era" ("The Day of Reckoning"), and, in particular, Ballard criticizes Channel Five's endless coverage of Nazism and Holocaust atrocities. Historical viewing of the "Hitler Channel," as Ballard referred to it, is compulsive, but it is also uncritical because all sense of historical specificity is emptied out by repeating surface images ("The Day of Reckoning"). As Rau notes, the proliferation of "fascism" has at least two significant consequences: firstly, our understanding of the "nature, mechanism and psychology of historical Nazism" is blocked by its cultural production; secondly, Nazism appears to operate as a "synecdoche for fascism" (4). Consequently, fascism is reduced to a "floating signifier" to which "any form of power or desire" can attach itself (3).

The idea of fascism as a floating signifier is one that *Kingdom Come* explores in an early moment of scene setting: "There were too many slogans and graffiti for comfort, too many BNP and KKK signs scrawled on cracked windows, too many St George's flags flying from suburban bungalows" (*KC* 16). On the surface, Brooklands appears to be a hot bed of neo-fascisms: namely, the British National Party, the National Front, the Klu Klux Klan, and the English Defence League (this latter group is signified throughout the novel by the ubiquitous symbol of the St George's Cross). If we accept this logic, it is reasonable to assume that *Kingdom Come* stages an imaginative enquiry into the survival of neo-fascisms within contemporary culture. Indeed, historians of fascism, such as Nigel Copsey, have long been alive to fascism's "capacity for creative mutation since 1945," and they argue for a much greater interrogation of the "continuities between historical fascisms and contemporary manifestations" (55) in order to better understand the complex political landscapes of the twenty-first century.

Certainly, *Kingdom Come* does invite this line of historico-political analysis. The novel is replete with inter-war and post-war historical references to fascist regimes and political dictatorships, from Italian fascism, Nazism and Stalinism to the totalitarian rule of Pol Pot in Cambodia and Juan Péron in Argentina. Notably, the overstated thesis of the novel – that consumerism is a new form of fascism – is developed in direct relation to these historical references, suggesting a continuity of sorts. Ballard's consumer fascism thesis is also propounded in extensive interview discussions, which, when taken together, seem to suggest that there are at least four interrelated elements in the consumer fascism model: the all-consuming and highly adaptable (and attractive) nature of consumer capitalism; the threat of elective psychopathology as an energizing response to the boredom of contemporary life; a profound masochistic strain running through modern industrial societies; and complicity. Ballard puts it like this:

> This is a collective enterprise. All of us who are members of consumer society; all of us are responsible. I think that these are sort of almost seismic movements that drift through the collective psyche and which facilitate the emergence of ultra-right-wing groups like the Nazis and the fascists in Italy.
>
> *EM* 419

Given such comments, it is hardly surprising that critics such as Holliday have made convincing cases for reading *Kingdom Come* as a Surrealistic exploration into whether "modern consumer society can mutate into something best understood in terms of 1930s Nazi Germany" (Holliday "Another Look at *Kingdom Come*"). If this is what *Kingdom Come* is suggesting, then it keeps company with Theodor Adorno's and Max Horkheimer's *Dialectic of Enlightenment*, which first elided the political models of Nazi Germany and American democracy, daring to explore them as variations of capitalism.

But there is always a but with Ballard. Even though *Kingdom Come* does encourage connections between historical fascisms, consumer fascisms and neo-fascisms, it also resists these connections precisely in those moments in which it appears to be making them. Just as the excess of neo-fascist insignia raises questions about whether this suburb of West London can really be home to the British National Party, the National Front, the English Defence League and the Klu Klux Klan, I also question the excess of analogies at work in *Kingdom Come*, most of which are deeply unsettling because they are so inappropriate:

> Illuminated arrays [from the Metro-Centre] glowed through the night
> like the perimeter lights of a colony of prison camps, a new gulag of penal
> settlements where the forced labour was shopping and spending.
>
> *KC* 78

> Take the Metro-Centre and its flat sales. Close your eyes a little and it
> already looks like a Nuremberg rally. The ranks of sales counters, the long
> straight aisles, the signs and banners, the whole theatrical aspect.
>
> *KC* 105

Ballard's use of analogy is odd and provocative. It is problematic enough to
collapse Stalinism and Nazism as *Kingdom Come* self-consciously does. But to
compare a shopping centre to the Gulag or retail techniques to the machinery
of Nazi propaganda is particularly troublesome. Yet *Kingdom Come* is replete
with bad analogies such as these. Other notable examples include overstated
evocations of *Kristallnacht* in a scene in which football supporters attack Asian
shopkeepers. Then, there are the reverse selections in the Metro-Centre, when
the hostages feign exhaustion so as not to be chosen for the clean-up opera-
tions. Conspicuously, these reverse selections take place in the chapter titled
"Work Sets you Free."

This is a pertinent point at which to briefly refer to De Chirico's interwar
novel, *Hebdomeros*, a favourite novel of Ballard's, which he identified as "one
of the seminal documents of surrealism."[1] Like *Kingdom Come*, *Hebdomeros* is
replete with unusual analogies and it opens in the middle of nowhere:

> And then began the visit to that strange building located in an austerely
> respectable but by no means dismal street. Seen from outside, the build-
> ing looked like a German consulate in Melbourne. Large shops took up
> the whole ground floor. Though it was neither a Sunday nor a holiday the
> shops were closed at the time, which gave to this portion of the street a
> weary, melancholy air, that particular dreary atmosphere one associates
> with Anglo-Saxon towns on a Sunday [...] The idea that the building re-
> sembled a German consulate in Melbourne was a purely personal one of
> Hebdomeros', and when he spoke about it to his friends they smiled and

---

1 Ballard endorsed De Chirico's novel: "One of the seminal documents of surrealism, *Hebdomeros* takes its place with Dali's *Secret Life* in the invisible library of the twentieth-century
imagination. Dreamlike, heroic and mysterious, *Hebdomeros* perfectly evokes the poetic and
twilight world of Chirico's greatest paintings." I am grateful to David Pringle for alerting me
to this.

said they found the comparison *odd*, but they immediately dropped the subject and went on to talk about something else [...] "It's strange," Hebdomeros was thinking, "as for me, the very idea that something had escaped my understanding would keep me awake at nights, whereas people in general are not in the least perturbed when they see or read or hear things they find completely obscure". (1)

Analogical thinking has always galvanized the Surrealist imagination. However, it received renewed emphasis in Breton's "Rising Sign" (1947), an essay written on return from exile, and as part of a broader post-war move to examine the legacies of totalising systems of language on the post-war critical consciousness. Although Breton advocates the playful, non-discursive energies of poetic analogy, this post-war, post-Holocaust essay is more concerned with poetic analogy's serious potential to mobilize thought against, what he calls, "the logical method, which has led us to our well-known impasse" (280). For Breton, this form of thought is "indifferent to anything that does not approach from very near," "insensible to anything that can deliver [...] an interrogation of nature," and dominated by the "most obtuse of detachments" (280). Breton's essay is provocative, and not least because of his own absence from actual political Resistance in fascist Europe. Nevertheless, *Hebdomeros* and *Kingdom Come* turn to analogical thinking in a similar move of critical seriousness in order to foreground a loss of critical engagement. As the long quotation suggests, in De Chirico's novel, Hebdomeros is something of an exception precisely because he is a tireless interrogator of enigmas, someone who works hard to uncover connections between the novel's strange and violent events whilst those around him form a languid and uncritical collective.

Kingdom Come is also home to a lazy critical collective, but, in contrast to De Chirico, Ballard presents his narrator as the main culprit. Over the course of the novel, Pearson shows himself to be a spectacularly bad reader of narrative events, and in this respect, Le Guin is quite right to label his narration "inadequate." As soon as Pearson makes an assumption of any kind the opposite shows itself to be the case. That said, I do not agree with Le Guin's conclusion that Pearson's affectless, monotone narration makes the reader question the very point of the novel. As James argues, Ballard's affectless late style is much closer to being "purposive" than it is poor writing: "It's a barometer registering the nullifying experiences he describes, showing syntactically how apathy eventually conditions his narrator's whole way of seeing" (166). Rather than dismiss Pearson's apathy as meaningless, then, perhaps the role of the reader is, like Hebdomeros, to interrogate the dynamics of what is actually being said. This is Pearson observing the shopping and sports-obsessed population of Brooklands,

> Waiting for the police to arrive, I followed this barely disciplined private army to a gypsy hostel beside a bus depot. The aggressive whistles and chanting terrified the exhausted Roma women trying to restrain their husbands. I left them to it.
>
> *KC* 126

> Sports-club stewards were a plague in the motorway towns, intimidating Asian and east European shopkeepers, harassing small businesses until 'voluntary' contributions were paid [...] I closed my mind to all this.
>
> *KC* 161

Pearson's decision to walk away from the first racist attack is less an indictment of it than an expression of indifference to, and complicity with, it. The detached observer-narrator does not even entertain the possibility of intervention. Similarly, his use of the term "voluntary" in the second quotation is telling because it shows that he is all too aware of the violent realties concealed within, and smoothed-over by, the linguistic gloss of euphemism. Turning away from repeated acts of racist violence and persecution, physically, psychologically and ethically, Pearson absolves himself from any sense of moral engagement or responsibility.

It is in behaviours such as these that *Kingdom Come* advances yet another model of fascism; namely micro-fascism. As Foucault warns in the Preface to *Anti-Oedipus*, the "major enemy" of the post-war period may be fascism, but it is not only "historical fascism, the fascism of Hitler and Mussolini – which was able to mobilize and use the desire of the masses so effectively" (xiii). It is "also the fascism in us all, in our heads and in our everyday behaviour, the fascism that causes us to love power, to desire the very thing that dominates and exploits us" (xiii). At stake in the concept of micro-fascisms is the recognition that fascism is not a discrete historical, geographical or political phenomenon that can be considered at a safe distance. Although fascist dynamics do continue to manifest themselves in marginal neo-fascist groups within contemporary culture, fascisms also survive *within* democracy; that is, they survive *within* the everyday behaviours and power relations that, as Adorno put it "reside beneath the smooth façade of everyday life" (90).

The concept of micro-fascisms is disturbing and compelling. Its resonance is evident in recent appropriations by contemporary historians and political scientists in their attempts to re-theorize fascism for the twenty-first century. Brad Evans and Julian Reid, for instance, open *Deleuze and Fascism: Security: War: Aesthetics* with a swift rejection of the post-war liberal imagination's "doubly political and moral claim to have somehow overcome fascism," clearing the way for their own disquieting thesis:

[W]e are concerned with interrogating contemporary power relations as predicated on the *real* and *necessary* existence of fascism [...] Fascism, we believe, is as diffuse as the phenomenon of power itself. Fascism is a problem [...] but it is not a problem we can solve [...] We believe in the necessity of accepting impurity as a condition of possibility for political thought and action. That means accepting that we are all, always fascists of multiple kinds. (1–5)

Reid and Evans's thesis holds well for a reading of micro-fascisms in *Kingdom Come*. Even though I have mainly focussed on Pearson's micro-fascistic behaviour in this discussion, it is something that every single character practises. For instance, Julia Goodwin, the resident doctor and co-architect of the murder of Pearson's father, departs the novel with a mock-fascist salute. Yet, the real danger lies in the admission she makes beforehand, namely that she can't say for sure that she would have behaved differently. Similarly, the threat of the spectators watching the Metro-Centre burn at the end of the novel does not reside in any kind of neo-fascist insignia they might adopt. Pearson tells us: "I watched the spectators around me, standing silently at the railing. There were no St George's shirts, but they watched a little too intently" (*KC* 280).

At the point at which *Kingdom Come* ends so many ambiguities survive. This is because Ballard's Surrealist imagination is not only prepared to accept that it inhabits the same territories as fascism and cannot, therefore, treat it as something Other or external; but it is also because Ballard recognizes that fascism is a problem that cannot be solved. As I have tried to show in my discussion of just five models of fascism in *Kingdom Come*, Ballard's final novel is alive to the threat and allure of fascism in all its forms. And if Evans and Reid are correct in suggesting that impurity *is* a necessary condition of possibility for political thought and action, then Ballard's art of analogy, which he takes up and develops from De Chirico, might just be one way in which Surrealism makes an imaginative contribution to debates on the problem.

Works Cited

Adorno, Theodor W. "The Meaning of Working Through the Past." *Critical Models: Interventions and Catchwords* [1959]. Translated by Henry W. Pickford. New York: Columbia University Press, 2005. 89–103.

Augé, Marc. *Non-places: Introduction to an Anthropology of Supermodernity* [1992]. Translated by John Howe. London and New York: Verso, 1995.

Ballard, J.G. "The Day of Reckoning." *The New Statesman*. Web. 20 April 2015.

Ballard, J.G. *"Kingdom Come*: An Interview with J. G. Ballard" with Jeannette Baxter. In *J. G. Ballard: Contemporary Critical Perspectives*. Ed. Jeannette Baxter. London: Continuum, 2008. 122–128.

Bataille, Georges. "The Labyrinth." *Visions of Excess: Selected Writing, 1927–1939*. Ed. and translated by Allan Stoekl. Minneapolis: University of Minnesota Press, 1994. 171–177.

Breton, André. "The Rising Sign." *What is Surrealism?: Selected Writings*. Ed. and translated by Franklin Rosemont. Part Three. New York: Monad Press 1978. 280–284.

Copsey, Nigel. "Fascism studies (and the 'Post-Fascist' era): an ideal meeting ground?" *Fascism: Journal of Comparative Fascist Studies* 1 (2012): 55–56.

De Chirico, Giorgio. *Hebdomeros: A Novel*. London: Peter Owen, 1992.

Evans, Brad and Julian Reid. *Deleuze and Fascism: Security: war: aesthetics*. London: Routledge, 2013.

Finkelstein, Haim. "'Deserts of Vast Eternity': J. G. Ballard and Robert Smithson." *Foundation* 39 (1987): 50–62.

Foucault, Michel. "Preface." Gilles Deleuze and Félix Guattari, *Anti-Oedipus: Capitalism and Schizophrenia* [1972]. London and New York: Continuum, 2004. Xi–xiv.

Franklin, Bruce. H. "What are we to make of J. G. Ballard's Apocalypse?" *Voices for the Future: Essays on Major Science Fiction Writers*. Edited by Thomas D. Clareson. Volume II. Bowling Green, Ohio: Bowling Green University Press. 1979. 85–105.

Gray, John. "Modernity and its Discontents." *The New Statesman*, 10 May 1999. Web. 17 June 2015.

Griffin, Roger. "Studying Fascism in a Postfascist Age. From New Consensus to New Wave?" *Fascism: Journal of Comparative Fascist Studies Fascism* 1 (2012): 1–17.

Harrison, M. John. "Narratives of the Mall." *The Times Literary Supplement*, 6 September 2006. Web. 21 April 2015.

Holliday, Mike. "A Fascist State?: Another Look at *Kingdom Come*." *Ballardian*, 7 July 2010. Web. 20 April 2015.

James, David. "Late Ballard." *J. G. Ballard: Visions and Revisions*. Edited by Jeannette Baxter and Rowland Wymer. London: Palgrave. 2012. 160–176.

Jewell, Keala. *The Art of Enigma: The De Chirico Brothers and the Politics of Modernism*. Pennsylvania: University of Pennsylvania Press, 2004.

Le Guin, Ursula. "Revolution in the Aisles." *The Guardian*, 9 September 2006. Web. 20 April 2015.

Luckhurst, Roger. *The Angle Between Two Walls: The Fiction of J. G. Ballard*. Liverpool: Liverpool University Press, 1997.

Rau, Petra. *Our Nazis: Representations of Fascism in Contemporary Literature and Film*. Edinburgh: Edinburgh University Press, 2013.

Stephenson, Gregory. *Out of the Night and into the Dream: A Thematic Study of the Fiction of J. G. Ballard*. London: Greenwood Press, 1991.

Index